84 -

110 - 116

W9-COS-551

THE SOVIET WOOD-PROCESSING INDUSTRY

A Linear Programming Analysis of the Role of Transportation Costs in Location and Flow Patterns

T

UNIVERSITY OF TORONTO DEPARTMENT
OF GEOGRAPHY RESEARCH PUBLICATIONS

THE SOVIET WOOD-PROCESSING INDUSTRY

A Linear Programming Analysis of the Role of
Transportation Costs in Location and
Flow Patterns

BRENTON M. BARR

Published for the University of Toronto,
Department of Geography
by the University of Toronto Press

Soc
HD
9765
R9
B34

LIBRARY
FLORIDA STATE UNIVERSITY
TALLAHASSEE, FLORIDA

© University of Toronto Department of Geography
Published by University of Toronto Press, 1970

Printed in Canada

ISBN 0-8020-3259-1

Published with the assistance of the University of Alberta and the Centre for
Russian and East European Studies, University of Toronto.

To Nina, Helen, and Rubie

Preface

The question is often raised concerning Western studies of the
Soviet Union: "Has this work already been done, or is it currently being done, in a more thorough fashion by Soviet scholars
themselves?" The question is a valid one. At least some Soviet research in the economic field is still regarded as confidential, necessitating parallel or similar work to be carried out
in the West. Other work is carried out in such a fashion that it
probably would not be undertaken by Soviet scholars at any time.
This study is an example of geographic research, which rear-
ranges the standard Soviet scheme of regional classification
and then proceeds with non-Marxian analysis of spatial location.
Systematic study of the geographic distribution of the wood-
processing industry has received recent Soviet attention, yet the
results have been rather disappointing and limited.[1] In general,
wood-processing has received attention by geographers as a
small chapter or section in a general book on the distribution of
industry or productive forces. Foresters and economists have
treated the location of the industry in a more satisfactory and
comprehensive manner. However, Soviet work has tended to
be descriptive and lacking in critical analysis of the location
problem. In particular, there has been little, if any, attempt
to assess the geographic distribution of the industry within the
general context of location theory and to evaluate the role played
by individual location factors. Knowledge of the Soviet wood-

[1]A full review of the literature is contained in B. M. Barr, "The Role of Transfer Costs
in the Location and Flow Patterns of the Soviet Wood-Processing Industry" (unpublished
Ph.D. dissertation, Department of Geography, University of Toronto, 1968), pp. 14-20.

processing industry in the West is scanty, reflecting the lack of materials in translation, the scarcity of good materials to translate, and the general lack of concern with the industry.

The use in this study of conversion factors to measure the output of all wood products in terms of roundwood equivalent is a departure from previous studies of the Soviet wood-processing industry. It is hoped that this technique will overcome traditional limitations in measuring regional location patterns for the wood-processing industry as a whole and evaluating the areal association between the processing industry and its raw material base. The same technique lays the groundwork for the analysis of optimum flow patterns between areas of surplus and deficit raw material.

The present monograph might also be viewed as a case study in the application of linear programming techniques to the analysis of transportation patterns within the wood-processing industry. Similar work has not been done by Soviet geographers. Although mathematical techniques have begun to be applied to the transportation problem by economists in the USSR since 1962, progress to date has been slow. In the isolated cases where work has been done on wood-processing, the results have not been published and the method owes much to the work of American scholars.

Attempts to obtain the published Soviet solutions relating to the formulation of general transportation problems and the location of wood-processing plants reveal that certain aspects of this work are still confidential. Studies in North America of some of the factors of location in wood-processing have been carried out using conventional techniques for particular branches of the wood-processing industry.

It is hoped that the present work will add to North American studies both knowledge of the location of wood-processing industries per se and a better understanding of the factors which have influenced the location of wood-processing in the Soviet Union.

Brenton M. Barr
Edmonton, Alberta
December, 1969

Acknowledgments

The interest and enthusiasm of Professor Neil Field greatly aided completion of my doctoral dissertation from which this monograph is derived. As supervisor of my doctoral programme at the University of Toronto, Professor Field generously donated his time and experience. I wish also to express my appreciation to Professors Larry Bourne, Ian Burton, Leslie Curry, Donald Kerr, and Bruce MacDougall for their encouragement and advice during my stay in Toronto. Mr. J. Holowacz, of the Research Branch, Ontario Department of Lands and Forests, provided helpful assistance in obtaining and interpreting Soviet forestry data. Thanks are also due to Mr. J. Chesterman, University of Alberta, for his technical assistance.

Financial support from the Centre for Russian and East European Studies at the University of Toronto, and from the Canada Council, permitted an extended visit to the USSR in 1967. Fellowships were generously provided by the Canada Council and the Government of the Province of Ontario during preparation of the doctoral dissertation. Although many people have assisted with preparation of this monograph, responsibility for errors, omissions or opinions expressed is solely that of the author.

I am deeply obliged to Mrs. Lydia Burton and her staff for their efforts in guiding the manuscript through the numerous stages which separate a manuscript from its published form.

I am very grateful to the University of Alberta for a major grant in aid of publication. The Centre for Russian and East European Studies, University of Toronto, also contributed to the cost of publication.

Contents

Tables

xiii

Figures

THE SOVIET WOOD-PROCESSING INDUSTRY

A Linear Programming Analysis of the Role of
Transportation Costs in Location and
Flow Patterns

I

Introduction

INDUSTRIAL LOCATION
IN A PLANNED ECONOMY

An underlying assumption of this study is that the most favourable location for industry in the Soviet Union is one which minimizes total costs. In the West, the assumption is often made that the most favourable location for an industry is one which maximizes profits. The latter assumption is quite realistic, when used with qualifications, in a competitive situation where no one producer has achieved minimum costs, and where the measure of suitable location is a relative one, based upon financial return relative to a competitor. In the Soviet Union, however, prices and costs are predetermined. Profit maximization comes by inducing directors and managers to reduce costs below established norms once a plant is in operation. A location which would maximize profits (i.e., ensure greatest benefit to a centrally administered economy) would in fact be a location at which costs were minimal.[1] Maximum benefit to

---

[1] Gosplan (the State Planning Commission) is currently preparing to calculate optimal plans for all sectors and types of production by minimizing costs with needs as given (Ekonomicheskaya Gazeta, No. 25 [1968], p. 11). (The transliteration system in this work corresponds to the basic form recommended in Soviet Geography: Review and Translation.) The assumptions expressed here were confirmed during an interview with representatives of the Sloka Pulp and Paper Mill in Latvia on June 30, 1967.

the state, therefore, is obtained through the location at which aggregate costs are minimal or near-minimal. Such a location involves the most economic combination of capital, labour, equipment, and resources. The extent to which central policies have led to locations which do not conform to this basic assumption could be evaluated if sufficient data were available.

In a centrally-administered economy such as that found in the USSR, it is assumed that adherance to a location requiring an optimum combination of inputs of capital, labour, and equipment is desirable. In a weight-losing industry such as wood-processing, where shipment of processed goods instead of raw materials means considerable savings, the factors—labour and energy costs, economies of scale, and planning policies—should exert an influence on the location of production to the extent to which their individual or cumulative savings compensate for increased transport costs. It is assumed, therefore, that Soviet planners do not deliberately allow the location of wood-processing at any point where transport expenditures are higher than elsewhere unless the need for such additional expenditures can be credited to other factors.

Deviation from a locational pattern in which the greatest savings in transport costs occur can be expected if the savings incurred are greater than the additional transport costs. This point is reinforced by Lösch in the following example:

> If for example, local wage differences are to be considered, we can indicate . . . by how much the labour cost per unit is greater or less than at the point of lowest freight costs. Instead of at the place of lowest freight costs, the plant will then be set up where the saving in wages less the additional freight costs is greatest. [2]

In the Soviet Union, where the national economy is the beneficiary of a location in which total costs are minimized, the location of all production should be related to a need for national saving in budgetary expenditures. Even if a particular location is the result of, for example, determined political policy to develop a backward region, all location decisions, even in such a rigid centralized economy, cannot be made on non-economic grounds. The cost to the national economy of many uneconomic locations will be higher than necessary and will prevent the

---

[2]A. Lösch, The Economics of Location, trans. by W. G. Woglom and W. F. Stolper, p. 25.

maximum return on investment funds. Consequently, the maximum possible industrial output from each unit of invested capital will not be achieved. This is closely related to the economic policies guiding individual plants as well. A location where costs are not minimal does not have as much importance to the financial success of Soviet enterprises as it does to Western enterprises. The Soviet state will not permit a plant to go bankrupt, and high production costs will not result in abnormally high prices or in reduction of sales. High costs will be absorbed by the national economy. This form of "subsidy," however, if aggregated for many industrial enterprises, results in high total national production costs which bear directly on the effectiveness of national investment plans.

In view of the increasing complexity of the Soviet economy and the apparent similarity of its economic difficulties to those of Western countries, it is no longer possible to conclude that the Soviet economy can afford to tolerate the location of industry where inputs are not near the minimum. It is essential, therefore, that concepts which are applicable to industry in competitive or demand economies should be applied, where relevant, to economic systems which appear superficially to be quite different.

The locational orientation of the wood-processing industry shows the influence of weight-loss of materials during processing and as such is a demonstration of a locational process first clearly described by Alfred Weber in his "Theory of the Location of Industries."[3] In the context of the wood-processing industry, Weber's theory suggests that, in terms of the weight of the major raw material, the weights of the other materials, amount of weight-loss in processing and thus weight of the resultant product, the industry will locate so as to minimize total transportation cost. The weight-loss problem has been considered by Hoover for the beet-sugar, naval stores, cotton-seed crushing, canning and preserving industries in the United States.[4] Weight-loss, however, remains a relatively uninvestigated factor in industrial location. The absence of concern for this factor in existing studies of the location of wood-processing is surprising in view of the overwhelming predominance of roundwood as a raw material, and the major loss in weight of roundwood during many forms of wood-processing.

[3]C. J. Friedrich, ed., Alfred Weber's Theory of the Location of Industries.
[4]Edgar M. Hoover, The Location of Economic Activity, pp. 31-35.

5

Analysis of the spatial organization of raw-material and product flows is also an integral part of the analysis of industrial location. The introduction in recent years of linear programming to spatial analysis has resulted in major advances in solution of the problem of optimum industrial location. Application of a specific aspect of linear programming, the so-called "Transportation Problem," first by Hitchcock and Koopmans and subsequently by such scholars as Abouchar, Fox, Goldman, Henderson, Koch, Snodgrass, Morrill and Garrison, permits derivation of an optimum pattern of flows between places of supply and demand, based on a minimum aggregate transportation cost.[5] The utility of the Transportation Problem has been demonstrated by analysis of flows of such industrial and agricultural commodities as ships, coal, cement, ketchup, wheat, flour, and livestock feeds. A recent study by Bruce[6] has applied the Transportation Problem to the shipment of lumber from the eleven western states in the USA to markets in the east. The study, completed in draft form in mid-1968 after lengthy preparation by over 15 contributors, is a major new step in the empirical application of the Transportation Problem on a regional basis to the American lumber industry. The primary objective was to determine if the transportation costs of marketing western lumber are minimal. In the present work, flow patterns in both lumber _and_ roundwood are assessed for all regions of the USSR. In both studies, it was found that the actual costs of total lumber transportation exceed the optimal minimal costs by at least 12 per cent. Optimal and actual flow patterns appear to differ in both the USA and the USSR for the same general reasons: a greater complexity of lumber species in reality than

[5]F. L. Hitchcock, "The Distribution of a Product from Several Sources to Numerous Localities," Journal of Mathematics and Physics, XX (1941), 224-230; T. C. Koopmans, "Optimum Utilization of the Transportation System," Cowles Commission Papers, New Series, No. 34 (1951), 136-146; A. Abouchar, "Rationality in the Prewar Soviet Cement Industry," Soviet Studies, XIX (1967), 211-231; K. A. Fox, "A Spatial Equilibrium Model of the Livestock-Feed Economy in the United States," Econometrica, XXI (1953), 547-566; T. A. Goldman, "Efficient Transportation and Industrial Location," Papers and Proceedings of the Regional Science Association, IV (1958), 91-106; J. M. Henderson, The Efficiency of the Coal Industry: An Application of Linear Programming (Cambridge: Harvard University Press, 1958); A. R. Koch and M. M. Snodgrass, "Linear Programming Applied to Location and Product Flow Determination in the Tomato Processing Industry," Papers and Proceedings of the Regional Science Association, V (1959), 151-162; R. L. Morrill and W. L. Garrison, "Projections of Interregional Patterns of Trade in Wheat and Flour," Economic Geography, XXXVI (April, 1960), 116-126.

[6]R. W. Bruce, Interregional Competition in Lumber Markets of the Eleven Western States (Unpublished manuscript, Review Copy, Washington State University, 1968).

accounted for in the model; the established connection between certain purchasers and sellers; product differentiation; the urgency of demand in which small differences in purchase price are ignored; and the seasonal availability of supplies whereby the optimum supplier may be out of stock. Two factors which appear further to complicate the actual situation in the United States are (1) the greater degrees of convenience and flexibility of using trucks rather than railways which may result in a non-optimum decision to use the former, and (2) the sale of "loss leaders" to expand sales in more profitable items. In the present study, the effect of both these factors in the USSR was not determined, but it is probable that in some form or other they may tend to influence the actual distribution of lumber.

In Bruce's study, an attempt was also made to determine if changing production, freight rates, and population are associated with changing market opportunities for western lumber producers. This hypothesis was accepted as true. Thus, the study of the eleven western states evaluates changes of the three key variables through time whereas this study of the USSR evaluates data for only 1964. However, this study analyzes in detail features ignored by Bruce: the structure of freight rates, the significance of weight-loss, and the interregional shipment of roundwood. Both studies complement each other and reveal the universal applicability of linear programming to the lumber industry as well as the general shortcomings inherent in a static model. These studies are indicative of the increasing empirical application of the Transportation Problem in geography and spatial economics to problems involving a large number of origins and destinations. The use of this aspect of linear programming in empirical studies involving many regions has been made feasible by the widespread availability of high-speed and large capacity computers in North America.

The application of linear programming in this analysis is intended to serve as another test of the general usefulness of the Transportation Problem in empirical research as well as to assess the utility of the technique to a hitherto unstudied situation— the Soviet wood-processing industry. It should be noted as well that this is an investigation of the aggregate location patterns of the Soviet wood-processing industry, not of the factors associated with the location of individual plants. Thus, though aspects of location in a planned economy are considered, the nature and significance of the decision-making process are not.

7

To evaluate the importance of transport costs in the spatial organization of Soviet wood-processing, it is necessary (1) to describe the location of wood-processing activity, the forest resource, and the market for wood-products, and to analyze the degree of areal association between the three patterns, (2) to measure the movement of roundwood and relevant wood-products and to relate actual to theoretical flow patterns, and (3) to evaluate the structure of Soviet rail tariffs, with reference to the dual problem of location of the processing industry and its interregional commodity flows.

MAJOR LOCATIONAL FACTORS

Transport Costs

Transportation costs are of special significance to the location of industry if their application has an important effect on the movement of either raw materials or finished products. If raw-material costs account for a large portion of the costs of production, and if a large portion of the weight of the raw material is lost during processing, then processing should occur close to the original source of supply. Significant transport savings are obtained when the maximum possible bulk or weight of a good is reduced before shipment. The magnitude of these savings increases with distance. The attraction of a raw-material location will, therefore, increase as distance between market and raw material increases.

The transport costs could, however, lead to location away from a raw material source if the cost of shipping finished goods per unit of weight substantially exceeded the freight rate on raw materials. In Canada, for example, freight rates per ton usually increase with the value of the commodity being handled (i.e., the rates include the concept of "what the traffic will bear"). The relative attraction of a raw material versus a market location will, therefore, depend on the magnitude of the weight loss in processing and the rate differential between raw materials and finished goods. Weight-loss and the structure of freight rates influence the location of wood-processing since the conversion of roundwood into processed items such as lumber, pulp, and paper involves considerable loss of weight and a substantial increase in value. The weight-loss during production of lumber, pulp, paper, and paperboard is discussed in detail in chapter ii.

Other Influences on Location

Despite the apparent overwhelming role of transport costs in the location of wood-processing, other factors may also be of importance in particular cases.

Labour. The wood-processing industry is not likely to be labour-oriented since labour costs comprise a small part of total costs. If it is assumed that wages are uniform and labour is equally available elsewhere, labour costs should not influence location. On the other hand, if labour were twice as expensive in areas of raw material supply as in the major market areas, then this factor could exert some regional influence on location. However, location would be affected only insofar as the savings in the wage bill were sufficient to offset increased costs of other factors, particularly those associated with transportation.

Capital costs. The cost of providing an economic infrastructure and social and domestic services in resource regions is higher than in many other Soviet areas which have had these items paid for in conjunction with development of other industries. In northern and eastern regions, construction of these features often is warranted by the development of wood-processing plants. Adequate housing and transportation facilities, for example, are usually available in long-settled areas of European Russia whereas developments in wood-processing often are located in areas of relatively recent exploitation. In some cases, the influence of capital costs on location may encourage location away from the raw material in order to save the high initial costs on investment in virgin territory.[7]

Energy. No single region has such an advantage in the supply of energy as to cause a major imbalance in wood-processing although Central Siberia now has the cheapest fuel and electricity costs in the USSR (Table 1). Areas of raw material supply in the USSR tend to have the lowest energy costs which appear to reinforce transport costs by further enhancing the attraction of a raw-material orientation.

Economies of scale. The role of economies of scale is not relevant to this study because the number and size of lumber, pulp, or paper mills in each region is not being investigated.

---

[7]Nikolaev has recently discussed the influences of the level of development in a region. "In the older regions, there exist unused labour resources which were provided with housing and public facilities. By contrast, in the newer regions, similar conditions seldom exist. Moreover, by including these ancillary expenditures, account can be taken of the factors which influence the construction costs of housing and public facilities" (S. Nikolaev, "Principles of Construction for an Interzonal Model in a Soviet Setting," Papers, Regional Science Association, XX [1968], 139).

TABLE 1. REGIONAL COSTS OF ENERGY IN THE USSR, 1964

| Regions | Full Production Costs (Regional Averages) of: | | | |
| | Thermal Energy | | Electricity | |
	Rubles/GKAL	Per Cent of USSR Average	Kopeks/KWH	Per Cent of USSR Average
USSR	2.70	100	.788	100
RSFSR	2.71	100	.734	93
Northwest	4.24	157	.760	97
European North	N.A.		N.A.	
Centre	3.54	131	.926	118
Volga-W. Urals	2.66	99	.807	104
Black Earth	N.A.		N.A.	
S. Volga	2.48	92	.643	82
Urals	2.38	88	.661	84
W. Siberia	2.55	94	.612	78
C. Siberia	1.78	66	.463	59
Far East	N.A.		N.A.	
Siberian North	N.A.		N.A.	
N. Caucasus	N.A.		.863	109
Southwest	2.48	92	.846	107
West	3.42	127	1.234	157
Caucasus	2.54	94	.874	111
Central Asia	N.A.		1.201	153

SOURCE: A. Ya. Avrukh, Problemy Sebestoyimosti Elektricheskoy i Teplovoy Energy, pp. 285-286, 295.

It is probable that the resource in all regions could support efficient sawmills of various scales and that most resource regions could support large mills. Economies of scale appear to have some relevance, however, in the distribution of pulp and paper production where the regional demand by paper mills may not be sufficient to warrant production of all types of pulp near paper mills. This is especially evident where heavy input of groundwood pulp is combined with small amounts of chemical pulp. Because the requirement for the latter is less than that required to make the production of pulp economical, chemical pulp may be shipped to various paper mills from one chemical pulp mill.

Inertia. Inertia is partly a function of administrative priorities in capital investment and partly a result of external economies arising from political events. In a strict economic sense, the Soviet Union obtained plants in the Baltic republics and Sakhalin free of charge and, apart from repairs or additions to capacity, was saved the necessity of allocating large sums to such projects. In a situation where the USSR was fortunate to

10

have <u>any</u> operational plants (after World War II), it was a relatively small matter to subsidize the high production costs at these sites by absorbing high transportation costs on the assembly of raw materials or distribution of products. High transport costs also appear to be accepted at plants where complete amortization of plant and equipment has been realized. The questions which must be asked here (although they cannot be answered) are, "How long can such a situation continue?" and "How much saving is actually being realized now?"

Inertia is also a result of heavy capital investment. Small sawmills show a more immediate response to changes in the cost of assembling roundwood as resources close to the mill are depleted. In fact, the logical solution by sawmills to changing assembly costs is achieved with the portable sawmill which permits more or less constant adjustment to the economics of wood assembly. Industries with high investment costs, such as pulp, paper, plywood, large sawmills, and integrated processing operations, usually are slow in responding to changing sources of raw materials. Soviet investment in the wood-processing industries has been rather haphazard, with the meagre funds available often being invested in spectacular projects such as those at Archangel, Balakhna, and Bratsk, while extended operation of plants which are inefficient and essentially, uneconomic, has often been encouraged. In a market economy, mills which have to undergo curtailment of raw material supplies or reduction in quality of raw materials are faced with the choice of perfecting newer and cheaper processing techniques, changing the output mix, or ceasing production. Price increases on products are possible insofar as higher prices do not adversely affect sales. In a monopoly situation, on the other hand, although constant technical and economic adjustments perhaps <u>should be made</u> in response to changes in raw material sources, adjustments are not mandatory.

The extra cost incurred on the transport of roundwood equivalent instead of finished products is one way of indicating the cost of inertia to the Soviet economy.

STATISTICAL UNITS FOR
LOCATIONAL ANALYSIS

One of the formidable problems facing the geographer using Soviet production statistics concerns the regional units em-

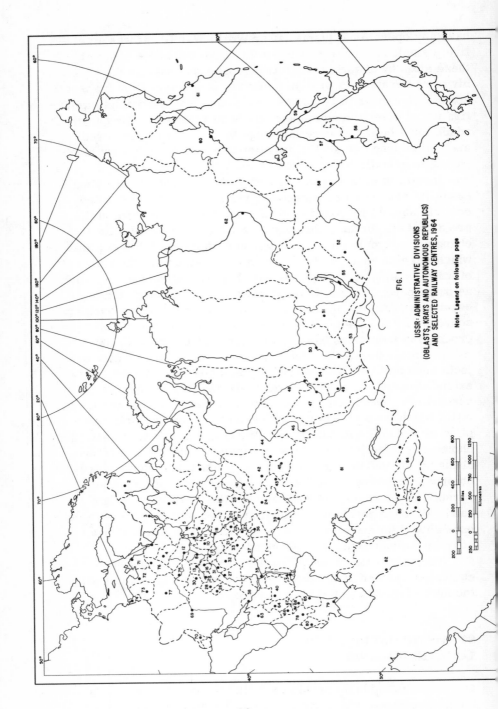

FIG. 1

USSR: ADMINISTRATIVE DIVISIONS
(OBLASTS, KRAYS AND AUTONOMOUS REPUBLICS)
AND SELECTED RAILWAY CENTRES, 1964

Note: Legend on following page

ENTRIES USED FOR MEASURING RAIL DISTANCES

Numbers correspond to divisions on Figure 1. The
order of numbers corresponds to the presentation of
oblast, kray, and ASSR data throughout the monograph.
Names in bold face type are regional aggregations used
in the study.)

ADMINISTRATIVE DIVISION	NUMBER ON MAP	RAIL CENTRE
NORTHWEST		
Leningrad obl.	1	Leningrad
Murmansk obl.	2	Kirovsk
Karelia ASSR	3	Medvezhegorsk
Novgorod obl.	4	Novgorod
EUROPEAN NORTH		
Vologda obl.	5	Vologda
Archangel obl.	6	Plesetsk
Komi ASSR	7	Ukhta
CENTRE		
Moscow obl.	8	Moscow
Yaroslavl obl.	9	Yaroslavl
Vladimir obl.	10	Vladimir
Ivanovo obl.	11	Ivanovo
Kalinin obl.	12	Kalinin
Kaluga obl.	13	Kaluga
Kostroma obl.	14	Galich
Ryazan obl.	15	Ryazan
Tula obl.	16	Tula
VOLGA--W. URALS		
Tatar ASSR	17	Kazan
Gorki obl.	18	Gorki
Kirov obl.	19	Kirov
Mari ASSR	20	Ioshkar-Ola
Mordovinian ASSR	21	Saransk
Chuvash ASSR	22	Kanash
Ulyanovsk obl.	23	Ulyanovsk
Bashkir ASSR	24	Ufa
Udmurt ASSR	25	Izhevsk
BLACK EARTH		
Belgorod obl.	26	Belgorod
Voronezh	27	Voronezh
Kursk obl.	28	Kursk
Orel obl.	29	Orel
Bryansk obl.	30	Bryansk
Lipetsk obl.	31	Lipetsk
Tambov obl.	32	Tambov
Penza obl.	33	Penza
S. VOLGA		
Astrakhan obl.	34	Astrakhan
Volgograd obl.	35	Volgograd
Kuybyshev obl.	36	Kuybyshev
Saratov obl.	37	Saratov
Rostov obl.	38	Rostov
Orenburg obl.	39	Orenburg
Kalmyk ASSR	40	Elista
URALS		
Perm obl.	41	Perm
Sverdlovsk obl.	42	Sverdlovsk
Chelyabinsk obl.	43	Chelyabinsk
Tyumen obl.	44	Tyumen
Kurgan obl.	45	Kurgan
W. SIBERIA		
Omsk obl.	46	Omsk
Novosibirsk obl.	47	Novosibirsk
Tomsk obl.	48	Tomsk
Altay kray	49	Half the distance- Barnaul and Biysk
C. SIBERIA		
Krasnoyarsk kray	50	Krasnoyarsk
Irkutsk obl.	51	Half the distance- Chita Tayshet;
Chita obl.	52	Chita Abakan Bratsk;
Tuva ASSR	53	Abakan Bratsk;
Kemerovo obl.	54	Kemerovo Tayshet-
Buryat ASSR	55	Ulan-Ude Tulun
FAR EAST		
Maritime kray	56	Iman
Khabarovsk kray	57	Khabarovsk
Amur obl.	58	Belogorsk
Sakhalin obl.	59	Uglegorsk
SIBERIAN NORTH		
Magadan obl.	60	Magadan
Kamchatka obl.	61	Ust'-Kamchatsk
Yakut ASSR	62	Yakutsk
NORTH CAUCASUS		
Krasnodar kray	63	Krasnodar
Stavropol kray	64	Stavropol
Dagestan ASSR	65	Makhachkala
Kabardinian-Balk. ASSR	66	Nal'chik
North Osetian ASSR	67	Ordzhonikidze
Chechen-Ingush ASSR	68	Grozny
SOUTHWEST		
Ukraine	69	Kiev
Moldavia	70	Kishinev
WEST		
Estonia	71	Tallin
Latvia	72	Riga
Lithuania	73	Kaunas
Kaliningrad obl.	74	Kaliningrad
Smolensk obl.	75	Smolensk
Pskov obl.	76	Pskov
Byelorussia	77	Minsk
CAUCASUS		
Georgia	78	Tbilisi
Azerbaydzhan	79	Baku
Armenia	80	Yerevan
CENTRAL ASIA		
Kazakhstan	81	Alma-Ata
Turkmenistan	82	Ashkhabad
Tadzhikistan	83	Dushanbe
Kirgizia	84	Frunze
Uzbekistan	85	Tashkent

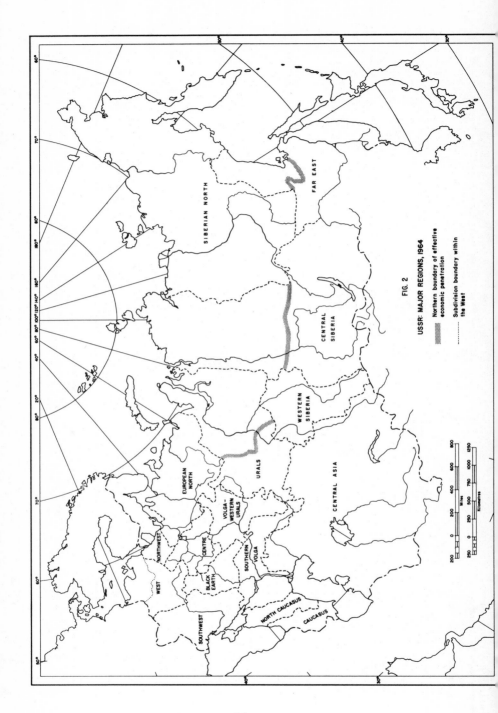

USSR: MAJOR REGIONS, 1964

FIG. 2

Northern boundary of effective economic penetration

Subdivision boundary within the West

14

ployed and the lack of consistency from one period to another.
The Soviet Union is divided along national and ethnic lines into
15 republics and most republics are further divided into oblasts (provinces), krays (territories), and autonomous republics.[8] These subdivisions are the basic statistical units for
reporting data in published reports. Lower level administrative units are seldom, if ever, used for reporting industrial
statistics. The chief difficulty in utilizing data from official
handbooks lies in the fact that oblast, kray, and autonomous
republic data are often aggregated into units termed "Large
Economic Regions." The number of these regions has changed
from period to period; the oblast composition has displayed remarkable variation, and the Large Economic Regions themselves
do not always correspond in regional makeup to the variation in
distribution of physical and economic phenomena on the earth's
surface. In order to obtain suitable regional units, the geographer often must arrange oblast, kray, and autonomous republic units in a system of his own creation. Rearrangements
of the regional subdivisions of the USSR are also necessary to
ensure comparability of basic units through time. The need for
this is brought about by the changing composition of Large Economic Regions and by the tendency to create or abolish certain
oblasts and autonomous republics.

The criteria used in this research to create a suitable regional system are (1) similarity in the type of forest resource,
(2) similarity in the nature of wood-processing, (3) areal con-
tiguity, and (4) sufficient difference from surrounding areas so
as to permit clear delineation of wood movements from supply
areas to areas of demand. The regional grouping of oblasts,
krays, and autonomous republics is illustrated in Figures 1 and
2.

The deviation of the system used here from other systems
is most noticeable in the western and northern parts of European Russia, the Urals, along the Volga river, and in Central
Siberia.

Manipulation and recording of data in preparation of the
study has occurred primarily at the level of the basic units —
oblasts, krays, and autonomous republics. This has permitted
accurate rearrangement of basic data to conform to other re-

[8]The term, "autonomous republic," is customarily designated by the abbreviation, ASSR.

15

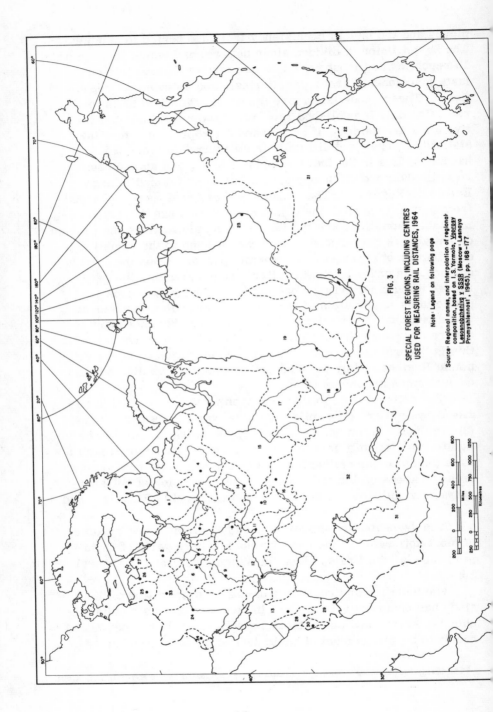

FIG. 3

SPECIAL FOREST REGIONS, INCLUDING CENTRES
USED FOR MEASURING RAIL DISTANCES, 1964

Note: Legend on following page

Source: Regional names, and interpolation of regional
composition, based on I. S. Yarmola, Voprosy
Lesonabzheniya y SSSR (Moscow: Lesnaya
Promyshlennost', 1965), pp. 168-177

gional systems when the need arose (Figure 3). An example of this is found in chapter v where a Soviet author's data on inter-regional movements of roundwood and lumber, using a regional system devised by that author, are compared with our basic data and are used for linear programming in a manner comparable with presentation of other data in the study. Adherance to one special regional system does not eliminate the possibility of subsequent regrouping of basic data to conform with future work done by this author or by other investigators of the Soviet scene.

Fig. 3. ·SPECIAL FOREST REGIONS, INCLUDING
CENTRES USED FOR MEASURING RAIL DISTANCES, 1964
(Numbers correspond to divisions on Figures 3, 7, 8, 9, and 10)

Region	Number on Map	Rail Centre
Northwest	1	Plesetsk
Leningrad	2	Novgorod
Murmansk	3	Kirovsk
Komi	4	Ukhta
Moscow	5	Moscow
Prioka	6	Kaluga
Upper Volga	7	Galich
Volga-Vyatka	8	Kanash
Central Black Earth	9	Voronezh
Mid-Volga	10	Ufa
Volga-Littoral	11	Kuybyshev
Lower-Volga	12	Volgograd
North Caucasus	13	Nalchik
Western Urals	14	Perm
Mid-Urals	15	Tyumen
Southern Urals	16	Chelyabinsk
Western Siberia	17	Tomsk
Kuzbass	18	Half the distance, Barnaul-Biysk
Krasnoyarsk	19	Krasnoyarsk
Eastern Siberia	20	Ulan-Ude
Khabarovsk	21	Belogorsk
Far East	22	Iman
North East	23	Sovetskaya Gavan'
Ukraine	24	Kiev
Lithuania & Kaliningrad	25	Kaunas
Latvia	26	Riga
Estonia	27	Tallin
Georgia	28	Tbilisi
Azerbaydzhan	29	Baku
Armenia	30	Yerevan
Central Asia	31	Tashkent
Kazakhstan	32	Alma-Ata
Byelorussia	33	Minsk
Moldavia	34	Kishinev

II

The Wood-Processing Industry

TERMS AND TECHNOLOGY

Industries producing wood products use a wide variety of techniques and processes. In this study, the industries selected
are representative of the mechanical and chemical processing
(or conversion) of raw wood into a product. Lumber represents
the former and pulp and paper collectively represent both, although the majority of pulp in the USSR is produced by chemical
processes. Products of these industries can be utilized as raw
materials in construction, service, and light industries (for
example, building frames, box manufacture, printing, publishing, and allied industries). The industries selected represent,
in general, examples of the primary conversion of wood (timber) into a product; the major raw material input is wood in the
form of roundwood or wood waste.

   Lumber is cut directly from round timber and does not require an intermediate stage of processing. Once cut, dried,
and perhaps planed, the timber is ready for consumption.
Waste from sawmilling can be utilized productively as fuel or
as the basis for manufacture of particle boards, laths, shingles,
cooperage, etc.[1] In this study, the particle board and fibre

---

[1]A. J. Panshin, et al., Forest Products, Their Sources, Production and Utilization, p.
248. Particle board is manufactured from small portions of whole wood in the form of
splinters, chips, flakes, or shavings. Fibre board is produced from mechanical pulp.

18

board industries are not analyzed and sawmilling waste will be considered only insofar as it acts as a raw material for pulp and paper production.[2]

Wood pulp is produced when logs are reduced to fibre by grinding (groundwood or mechanical pulp) or by cooking under pressure at high temperatures (chemical pulp). Different cooking solutions yield different types of pulp: calcium bisulphate (sulphite), caustic soda and sodium sulphide (sulphate or kraft), caustic soda (soda), etc. The type or mixture of pulp determines the character of the paper produced. Groundwood pulp, occasionally mixed with 20 per cent sulphite, is used primarily for producing newsprint. Alone, or with groundwood, soda, or rag pulp, unbleached sulphite is the chief raw material in all paper other than newsprint. Sulphate (Kraft) pulp is used for the production of wrapping paper, paper bags, container board, etc., which require strength. It is worth noting that "sulphate pulp constitutes 17 per cent of the total pulp production and 24 per cent of the total chemical pulp production of the USSR."[3] The distinction between chemical pulp and groundwood pulp is important because of the differing amounts of roundwood required for production of each type of pulp. Unfortunately, in Soviet statistics, one term, tsellyuloza, includes both chemical pulp for production of paper, and viscose pulp which is used to produce rayon and other chemical fibres, although the full amount of pulp used for non-paper purposes is not revealed.

Publication by region of statistics for the production of all kinds of pulp has been very limited in the USSR. Chemical pulp figures have not been published consistently for Major Economic Regions or Union Republics for the same years as figures for paper, plywood, and lumber. Regional production figures for groundwood (mechanical) pulp have not appeared at all in postwar statistical handbooks. These figures have had to be estimated from a combination of secondary sources which list some data for production of chemical pulp. For 1964, all pulp data have been estimated but the results are felt to be very reliable.[4] Moreover, pulp is simply a stage in the production of paper and

[2]Ibid.

[3]J. Holowacz, Opportunities for Export of Paper Bags to the USSR, p. 31.

[4]A new Soviet reference manual, published after completion of the analysis for this study, contains regional figures for production of chemical pulp in 1964. These figures correspond closely to estimates made here. A. Z. Katsenelenbaum, chief ed., Spravochnik Ekonomista-Bumazhnika.

much of the analysis of the location pattern of the pulp and paper industry focuses on the location of the paper industry. It is worth noting that recent development policy in the USSR has encouraged the construction of new capacity for production of pulp and paper at the same site.

Paper comes in many forms and can be derived from material other than wood, namely rags, reeds, and straw. Most paper, however, is made from pulp derived from roundwood or waste chips from other wood-processing industries. Paper is made from cellulose (usually derived from wood) by mixing the fibres with water, placing a layer of the mixture on a horizontal screen, draining off the water and leaving a thin mass of wet pulp. The remainder of the water is then removed by pressure and heat; the fibres "matt" or "felt" and become a compact sheet of paper. Paperboard, like paper, is available in various types and qualities and may be produced from any pulps or mixture of them.[5]

WEIGHT REDUCTION
DURING PROCESSING

The weight of roundwood dominates the weight of all other ingredients required for production of pulp and paper. Roundwood is the sole raw material required for production of lumber. The loss of weight during processing is so great that considerable savings in raw material assembly costs are achieved when transportation costs on roundwood are kept to a minimum. Although conditions vary from mill to mill, it is important nevertheless to present some idea of the magnitude of the loss in weight of roundwood during processing (Table 2).

The examples of weight losses during conversion of roundwood into pulp and paper, and pulp into paper, show the need, in most cases, for a location of processing activity close to the source of the chief raw material — roundwood.[6] Not all pulp

[5]These definitions follow very closely those provided by Mr. V. J. Raybould, Industrial Development Representative, British Columbia Hydro and Power Authority, Vancouver, B.C., in a personal communication to the author June 21, 1965.

[6]At the Balakhna pulp and paper mill, for example, the weight of sulphite pulp at the digester is comprised of 93.7 per cent of roundwood, 3.6 per cent sulphur products, and 2.7 per cent limerock. The total weight of ingredients for newsprint at Balakhna is 22.8 per cent chemical pulp, 74.0 per cent groundwood and 3.2 per cent kaolin. At the Visherskiy pulp and paper mill, 86.3 per cent of the weight of ingredients for production of writing paper is chemical pulp, the remaining 13.7 per cent being comprised of kaolin (Katsenelenbaum, Spravochnik, pp. 198-199).

20

and paper production in the USSR, however, is located at the site of roundwood supply, and not all paper mills produce sufficient pulp to meet their own requirements. Thus, the factor of weight-loss is a basic reason for locating pulp and paper production near sources of roundwood. However, location appears also to involve planning upsets caused by wartime dislocations and by economies of scale which necessitate certain specified production from various pulp machines even if all the pulp produced in the mill cannot be consumed there.

It should be noted in passing that the smaller weight-loss in the production of groundwood pulp than in the production of chemical pulp may not necessarily permit greater freedom in locating groundwood production away from sources of raw materials. The groundwood process requires approximately 4-5 times more electricity per ton of output than production of chemical pulp. Thus, chemical pulp mills have greater freedom than groundwood mills in locating away from sources of electricity.

TABLE 2. WEIGHT-LOSS IN THE WOOD-PROCESSING INDUSTRY

Product	Weight Lost in Production of 1 Ton of Product
Primary Conversion	
	(Per Cent of Roundwood-Requirement Lost Per Ton of Product)
Lumber (Coniferous)	49
Chemical Pulp	70
Groundwood Pulp	40
Paper	54
Paperboard	7
Secondary Conversion	
	(Per Cent of Pulp-Requirement Lost Per Ton of Product)
Newsprint (Balakhna)	7
Typographical Paper (Visherskiy)	25

SOURCE: The weight of roundwood was obtained from Economic Commission for Europe, and Food and Agriculture Organization, Joint Working Party on Forest and Forest Products Statistics, Conversion Factors, Annex II, pp. 1-2. The weight-loss for production of newsprint and typographical paper were calculated from Katsenelenbaum, Spravochnik, pp. 198-199.

21

CONVERSION FACTORS

Conversion of all production into roundwood requirement facil-
itates derivation of regional balances of supply and demand of
roundwood and provides a common denominator with which to
measure the relative magnitude of each branch of the wood-
processing industry in any region.

Conversion factors are general figures which vary between
species, regions, and countries. Each major forest region of
the world has its own conversion rates which reflect local tree
species and efficiency of wood utilization. Obviously, use of
the conversion factors peculiar to any national unit is desirable
when dealing with production of that national unit.

Official Soviet conversion factors for the Soviet forest industry, however, could not be obtained. Isolated examples for
particular regions or areas, found in published sources, were
not adequate for the purposes of this research. Application of
conversion factors used in other countries, for example, in
Canada and Great Britain, was not desirable because the precise
composition, by species, of Soviet roundwood consumption for
each region is not known. For most mechanical processing of
wood, conversion factors were derived from Soviet statistical
handbooks. When the national roundwood requirement for an
item and the total production of the item were known, the latter
could be divided into the former to derive an average ratio for
the country as a whole. Thus, in the case of lumber, the conversion factor so derived (which is lower than those provided
by other countries), probably reflects the Soviet custom of
producing considerable amounts of low-grade lumber. For
chemical pulp, paper, paperboard, fibreboard, and particle
board, however, official conversion factors, used by the United
Nations to compile international data, were found to be most
suitable, if not ideal, in converting Soviet production figures.
These conversion factors, in unpublished form, were supplied
by the UN. The UN uses general conversion factors in cases
where member governments such as the Soviet Union, have not
supplied national conversion factors. Use of these general
factors, however, apparently occurs with the implicit approval
of the government concerned. Some important conversion factors are compared in Table 3.

TABLE 3. CONVERSION FACTORS (Roundwood Equivalent)
(M³ [r])

Item	Unit	Estimated USSR[a]	Other[b]				
			(1)	(2)	(3)	(4)	(5)
Sawnwood	1 M³(s)	1.54			2.14(1.87)		1.67
Coniferous	1 M³(s)	1.54	1.67	1.67	2.14(1.87)		1.67
Broadleaved	1 M³(s)		1.82	1.82	2.14(1.87)	1.86	1.67
Sleepers	1 Piece	.235		.182			
	1 M³(s)	2.35	1.82	1.82	2.38	1.86	1.82
Plywood	1 M³	3.16	2.3	2.3		1.92	2.5
Particleboard	1 M³	1.3					
	1 Met ton	2.0	2.0	1.12		2.1	2.22
Fibreboard	1 M²	.0019					
	1 Met ton	2.0	2.0	2.0	2.0	2.5	
Groundwood Pulp	1 Met ton	2.5	2.5	2.55	2.65	2.5	2.55
Chemical Pulp	1 Met ton	4.9	4.9	4.6	5.31	4.6	5.04
Newsprint	1 Met ton	2.8	2.8	2.8	2.97	3.6	
Printing and Writing Paper	1 Met ton	3.5	3.5	3.5	3.65	4.2	3.65
All Paper	1 Met ton	3.2					
Other Paper	1 Met ton		3.25	3.25	3.65	4.3	4.0
Paperboard	1 Met ton	1.6	1.6	1.6	1.78	3.7	1.6

[a]Calculated from: See footnotes of Table 4.

[b]Official ECE/FAO (col. 1), United Kingdom (col 2), Canada, with B.C. in parenthesis (col. 3), US (col. 4), Ukraine SSR (col. 5). All columns from Economic Commission for Europe, and Food and Agriculture Organization, Conversion Factors, Annex I, Tables C and D; Annex II, Table 3. Conversion factors for Sawnwood and Sleepers in Column 2 are from Forestry Commission, Conversion Tables for Research Workers in Forestry and Agriculture, p. 30 (based on FAO factors).

UTILIZATION OF ROUNDWOOD

Utilization of roundwood in the Soviet Union in 1964 was still at an unsophisticated and rather primitive level. Far too great a percentage of Soviet roundwood is consumed in unprocessed form (round) or by industries using simple mechanical processes (sawmilling, railway-sleeper, and match production). In the leading industrial nations of Western Europe and North America, wood-processing is characterized by complex mechanical, and intensive chemical, utilization and conversion of roundwood. Gorovoy and Privalovskaya contend that, in 1959,

TABLE 4. UTILIZATION OF ROUNDWOOD IN THE USSR, 1964

Item	Output 1964	Conversion Factor	Roundwood Equivalent M^3 (r) x 10^3	Per Cent of Total
Primary				
Lumber-M^3 x 10^3	110,899.0	1.54[a]	170,784.46	61.7
Plywood-M^3 x 10^3	1,658.0	3.16[b]	5,239.28	1.9
Chemical Pulp-Tons x 10^3	2,933.0	4.9	14,371.70	5.2
Groundwood Pulp-Tons x 10^3	1,150.0	2.5[c]	2,875.00	1.0
Sleepers-Pieces x 10^6	50.1	4.25[d]	11,800.00	4.3
Matches-Crates x 10^6	15,228.0	18.8[e]	810.00[f]	.3
Subtotal— Major Processing Industries			205,880.44	74.4
Pit Props			20,000.00[g]	7.2
Tanning-Extractive Material			830.62[h]	.3
Material for Processing Acetic Acid			830.62[h]	.3
Poles			3,500.00[g]	1.3
Construction Wood and Poles over 7 cm			33,500.00[g]	12.1
Ship and Marine Lumber			2,400.00[g]	.9
Others			1,217.22	.4
Subtotal—Other Uses			62,278.46	22.5
Roundwood Export			8,736.00[i]	3.1
Roundwood Import			20.90[j]	
Net Roundwood Export			8,715.10	
TOTAL Roundwood			276,874.00	100.0
TOTAL Available for Consumption within USSR			268,158.90	
Secondary				
Paper-Tons x 10^3	3,033.2	3.2[k]	9,706.24	
Paperboard-Tons x 10^3	1,086.8	1.6	1,738.88	
Fibreboard-M^2 x 10^3	118,213.0	.0019[l]	224.60	
Particleboard-M^3	591,630.0	1.3[m]	769.12	

SOURCES: Unless otherwise noted, conversion factors are from Economic Commission for Europe, and Food and Agriculture Organization, Conversion Factors, Annex II, Table 3. Unless otherwise noted, production figures are from Narodnoye Khozyaystvo SSSR v 1964 godu, pp. 193-199.

[a]Soviet recovery figure given in Promyshlennost' SSSR, p. 299 is used. If the lumber produced came from 65 per cent of the log, then the roundwood requirement is: 110,899 x 1.54 = 170,784.46 M^3 (r).

[b]Figure derived from Promyshlennost' SSSR, pp. 295, 298.

[c]Figure for 1963, ibid., p. 302.

[d]Derived from ibid., p. 295, and Narodnoye Khozyaystvo RSFSR v 1964 godu, p. 89.

[e]Promyshlennost' SSSR, pp. 295, 298.

[f]Figure for 1963, ibid., p. 295.

[g]Figures for 1962, ibid., p. 295.

[h]Derived from I. S. Yarmola, Voprosy Lesosnabzheniya v SSSR, p. 33.

[i]Vneshnaya Torgovlya SSSR za 1964 god, p. 32.

[j]Ibid., p. 46.

[k]This figure is an average between newsprint (2.8) and writing paper (3.5), i.e., 3.2.

[1]1000 M^2 weigh .95 metric tons; 1 metric ton = 2M^3 roundwood equivalent. If .95
metric ton = 1000 M^2, 1.00 metric ton = $\underline{1.00 \times 1000}$ = 1,052.6M^2.
                                                    .95
Therefore: 1,052.6M^2 = 2M^3 roundwood equivalent; 118,213,000M^2 = $\underline{118,213,000 \times 2}$ =
                                                                              1,052.6
224,600 M^3 (r) or: 1M^2 = .0019M^3.

[m]1 metric ton of particleboard = 2.0 M^3 roundwood equivalent; 1M^3 of particleboard
= .65 metric tons. Therefore: 1 M^3 of particleboard = 2.0 M^3 (r) x .65 = 1.3M^3 (r).

5.6 per cent of the USSR's commercial roundwood was converted
into pulp while the relative figures for Western Europe and
North (and Central) America were 28.4 and 27.8 per cent respectively.[7] In Table 4, conversion factors have been employed
to determine the roundwood requirements of each sector of the
Soviet wood-processing industry in 1964. Utilization of roundwood in unprocessed form is also shown in the table. The pulp
and plywood industries consumed an estimated 8.1 per cent of
the roundwood supply, while processing by the lumber, sleeper,
and match industries consumed 66.3 per cent of the total. Approximately one-quarter of Soviet timber was consumed in unprocessed form or was exported.

Conversion of roundwood into lumber and pulp are the most
significant activities carried out in Soviet wood-processing.
These two activities account for over two-thirds of Soviet wood-
processing, while lumber production alone accounts for over
three-fifths of all Soviet processing. In the United States, more
than one-quarter of all commercial timber is subjected to
chemical processing while the figure for Canada is greater than
two-fifths.[8] The low figure of 6.2 per cent for conversion of
roundwood into all forms of pulp in the USSR is indicative of the
underdeveloped state of the entire wood-processing industry
relative to other leading industrial nations.

It should be noted that in Table 4, the figures for pulp production (4.08 million tons) correspond very closely with the
total figures for production of paper and paperboard (4.12 million tons), whereas there is a large discrepancy between the
two totals when the figures are converted into roundwood equivalent (17.24 million and 11.44 million, respectively). This
difference is partially caused by the utilization of dissolving

[7]V. L. Gorovoy and G. A. Privalovskaya, Geografiya Lesnoy Promyshlennosti SSSR,
p. 11.
[8]P. V. Vasil'yev, et al., Ekonomika Lesnogo Khozyaystva SSSR, p. 68.

pulp to produce artificial fibres (in 1963, 250,000 tons of dissolving pulp were produced),[9] and by the conversion factors used to convert paper and paperboard into roundwood equivalent. The significance of the difference is that the conversion factors used to determine the roundwood equivalent of paper and paperboard should probably be larger than those now used.

THE CHANGING SPATIAL
PATTERN OF THE INDUSTRY

Wood-Processing on
the Eve of Revolution

Wood-processing in 1913 occurred chiefly in the European regions of the Russian Empire at such important centres as Pinsk, Grodno, Kondrovo, Volgograd, Archangel, and Novaya Lyalya (northern Urals). Penetration of the extensive northern and eastern forests (away from the coast, rivers, and railways) had not begun. Many plants were oriented toward export by sea or rail.

In 1913, approximately four-fifths of the annual output of all wood-processing came from the Baltic, the North (Archangel), the Volga, and along the Dnieper.[10] Over one-third of all wood-processing activity was located in centres near the western border of Russia.[11] Sawmilling activity was located in or near the ports of Archangel, Riga, St. Petersburg (now Leningrad), and the basic riverways of the Volga and Dnieper.[12] Approximately nine-tenths of the sawn lumber was produced in European Russia, chiefly near the above locations. Plywood production was concentrated in the Baltic states (primarily in the cities of Tallin and Riga) and in Minsk oblast. Most of the plywood produced in Russia in 1913 came from these areas.[13] In 1913, 73.2 per cent of all paper was produced in the West, 18.4 per cent in the Centre and Black Earth, 6.5 per cent in the North and East, and the remaining 1.9 per cent probably in

[9] Lesnaya Promyshlennost', No. 148, 1963, p. 2.

[10] N. P. Nechuyatova, Geograficheskoye Razmeshcheniye Derevoobrabatyvayushchey Promyshlennosti SSSR, p. 7.

[11] Ibid.

[12] Ibid.

[13] P. N. Stepanov, Geografiya Promyshlennosti SSSR, p. 204.

the South.[14] Except for the production in the North and East,
most paper production was located in those areas which are
recognized today as being wood-deficit regions.

Expansion of the wood-processing industries in the Soviet
era, therefore, started from a very limited base in the western and central regions of European Russia.

Lumber Production, 1940-1964

Throughout 25 years involving a catastrophic war and cataclys-
mic general industrial growth, the Russian republic has consistently produced four-fifths of all Soviet lumber (Table 5).
Until 1960, all regions and republics of the Soviet Union registered an absolute growth in lumber production suggesting official failure to curtail production in those areas where logging
exceeds the annual allowable cut. By 1964, however, a slight
decrease in production was noticeable within the RSFSR in the
Black Earth, Southern Volga, and North Caucasus regions,
and in all regions outside the RSFSR except Central Asia.

Since 1940, all but four out of twelve regions within the
RSFSR have declined or stayed more or less the same in relative importance. Only one region, Central Siberia, has shown
a constant increase in relative importance while the share of
the Volga-Western Urals, Black Earth, and Siberian North regions in 1964, although greater than in 1940, was smaller than
(or, in the case of the North Caucasus, the same as) the relative share in intermediate years. These observations do not
confirm that a significant redistribution of the Soviet lumber
industry has occurred in the past 25 years as general Soviet
statements have suggested. Although the share of Central
Siberia in total Soviet production has increased from 9 to over
15 per cent, the absolute increase in production is less than
one-fifth of the increase in total Soviet output. Moreover, the
growth of sawmilling during this period in Central Siberia appears to have been at the expense of West Siberia and the Far
East, which have declined relative to total national production
since 1940. Thus, a modest trend can be observed away from
European Russia towards Central Siberia. In total, however,
the record of relocation is not very encouraging considering
the many statements made concerning its desirability. Even

[14]Ibid., p. 207.

TABLE 5. DISTRIBUTION OF LUMBER PRODUCTION (M³ x 10³)

Regions	1940	Per Cent	1956	Per Cent	1960	Per Cent	1964	Per Cent
USSR	35,438	100.0	76,583	100.0	105,556	100.0	110,899	100.0
RSFSR	28,755	81.1	60,616	79.1	83,568	79.2	90,189	81.3
Northwest	2,906	8.2	4,896	6.4	6,923	6.6	7,313	6.6
European North	4,111	11.6	6,941	9.1	9,354	8.9	10,565	9.5
Centre	3,255	9.2	6,478	8.5	8,714	8.2	9,694	8.7
Volga-W. Urals	3,631	10.2	9,516	12.4	13,002	12.3	12,698	11.5
Black Earth	672	1.9	1,444	1.9	2,460	2.3	2,416	2.2
S. Volga	1,755	4.9	3,237	4.2	4,824	4.6	4,484	4.0
Urals	4,115	11.6	9,510	12.4	12,146	11.5	12,739	11.5
W. Siberia	1,913	5.4	3,218	4.2	4,047	3.8	4,722	4.3
C. Siberia	3,201	9.0	9,606	12.5	13,683	13.0	16,799	15.1
Far East	2,324	6.6	3,228	4.2	4,306	4.1	4,744	4.3
Siberian North	196	.6	517	.7	783	.7	810	.7
N. Caucasus	505	1.4	1,357	1.8	2,294	2.2	2,233	2.0
Southwest	3,000	8.5	7,856	10.3	10,977	10.4	9,746	8.8
West[a]	3,038	8.6	5,758	7.5	7,076	6.7	6,772	6.1
Caucasus	387	1.1	871	1.1	1,497	1.4	1,215	1.1
Central Asia	429	1.2	2,150	2.8	3,470	3.3	3,949	3.6

SOURCE: Narodnoye Khozyaystvo RSFSR v 1958 godu, pp. 116–118; Narodnoye Khozyaystvo SSSR v 1958 godu, p. 255; Narodnoye Khozyaystvo RSFSR v 1964 godu, pp. 95–96; Narodnoye Khozyaystvo SSSR v 1964 godu, p. 197.

[a]The West includes Kaliningrad, Pskov, and Smolensk oblasts of the RSFSR.

28

in areas outside the Russian republic, relative decline in the share of national production since 1940 is noticeable only in the West. The conclusion must be drawn, therefore, that the location pattern of lumber production has purposely been maintained and that investment in plant and facilities in new areas has been given a very low priority. The situation probably also reflects difficulties in fulfilling plans for construction of new sawmills and integrated processing plants in such new areas as the European North, the Urals, and Central Siberia.

Paper Production

Production of paper in the Soviet Union has traditionally been concentrated in four regions—the Northwest, Volga-Western Urals, Urals, and the West. Developments since 1940 have not seriously altered this concentration although the Volga-Western Urals, and to a lesser extent, the Northwest, have declined relatively while the Urals and West have slightly increased their share. Collectively, the four regions accounted for about 70 per cent of the nation's paper production in 1964. Unlike lumber production, paper production has continued to increase absolutely in every area since 1960, although in varying proportions (production does not occur in the Siberian North or in the North Caucasus). Although the largest absolute increases in production have been registered within the RSFSR in regions of sufficient resource potential, it is evident that preference has been accorded regions which are close to the European market area (see Table 6). Thus, the Northwest, European North, Volga-Western Urals, and Urals have apparently been given preference over large-scale expansion in Central Siberia and the Far East. Despite the publicity given to spectacular projects at Krasnoyarsk, Bratsk, and Selenga, expansion in Central Siberia has not approached the level which was prophesied for the late 1960's a decade ago. Growth in the Far East, of smaller magnitude than elsewhere, has nevertheless been sufficient to keep that region in fourth place in paper production within the RSFSR and in fifth place for the country as a whole. It is surprising that growth has occurred at all in view of the fact that production far exceeds the demand for paper within the region. The Far East paper production is an anomaly, of course, as the Soviet Union inherited the paper

TABLE 6. DISTRIBUTION OF PAPER PRODUCTION (Tons x 10^3)

Regions	1940	Per Cent	1956	Per Cent	1960	Per Cent	1964	Per Cent
USSR	838.4	100.0	1,993.5	100.0	2,420.8	100.0	3,033.2	100.0
RSFSR	690.6	82.4	1,616.9	81.1	1,940.8	80.2	2,471.0	81.5
Northwest	222.8	26.6	428.8	21.5	529.7	21.9	707.9	23.3
European North	51.4	6.1	115.7	5.8	142.1	5.9	190.9	6.3
Centre	60.1	7.2	98.2	4.9	113.0	4.7	120.4	4.0
Volga–W. Urals	159.9	19.1	256.6	12.9	273.9	11.3	332.3	11.0
Black Earth	14.3	1.7	23.8	1.2	36.3	1.5	40.6	1.3
S. Volga	14.1	1.7	19.0	1.0	22.7	.9	51.0	1.7
Urals	154.6	18.4	439.2	22.0	507.1	20.9	596.3	19.6
W. Siberia	.7	.1	1.2	.1		.1	1.9	.1
C. Siberia					9.9	.4	88.2	2.9
Far East			150.5	7.5	197.0	8.1	215.0	7.1
Southwest	27.9	3.3	103.2	5.2	147.4	6.1	174.6	5.8
West[a]	108.3	12.9	320.9	16.1	397.1	16.4	466.2	15.3
Caucasus	9.7	1.2	29.6	1.5	33.7	1.4	36.4	1.2
Central Asia	1.9	.2	6.8	.3	9.5	.4	11.5	.4

SOURCE: Narodnoye Khozyaystvo RSFSR v 1958 godu, p. 123; Narodnoye Khozyaystvo SSSR v 1958 godu, p. 257; Promyshlennost' RSFSR, p. 186; Narodnoye Khozyaystvo RSFSR v 1964 godu, p. 101; Narodnoye Khozyaystvo SSSR v 1964 godu, p. 199.

[a]The West includes Kaliningrad, Pskov, and Smolensk oblasts of the RSFSR.

plants in southern Sakhalin oblast from the Japanese. Completion of a large plant at Komsomolsk will help maintain the relative standing of the Far East in total paper production but will not increase it.

On the other side of the Soviet Union, the USSR inherited large paper-making capacity in 1940 with the take-over of the three Baltic republics, and in 1945, with the inclusion of Kaliningrad (formerly Königsberg) into the country. All four areas are significant producers of paper although, unlike the Far East, they are deficient in timber supplies.

The relative share of the European North, Southern Volga, Western Siberia, and the Caucasus regions was the same in 1964 as in 1940, although minor fluctuations are evident in intervening years. Total production in the Southwest is still rather modest, but the area has increased its relative standing. Although production should be expected to increase in a region such as the European North, growth in the Southwest (the Ukraine) comes as a surprise in view of the heavy imports of roundwood into the region.

Changes in the distribution of paper production thus reveal several trends which appear to be working at cross-purposes. It is evident that the largest absolute increases have occurred in areas with adequate forest reserves (the Northwest and the Urals), but considerable gains have been made in the resource-deficient regions of the West and Southwest. In the case of the two areas inherited after 1940—the West and the Far East—production has not only continued but has actually increased, although certain diseconomies appear to be potentially very significant.

Paperboard Production
The distribution of paperboard production displays the same type of distribution as lumber and paper production in that several regions account for a large share of national output. The relative importance of the RSFSR, however, is much less in total Soviet paperboard production than in the other two industries.

Every producing region in 1940 registered absolute increases in the 25 years prior to 1964. Relative changes, however, have been drastic in many cases. The three regions (Northwest, Centre, and Volga-Western Urals) within the RSFSR of primary importance in 1940 had decreased in rela-

31

TABLE 7. DISTRIBUTION OF PAPERBOARD PRODUCTION[a] (Tons x 10³)

Regions	1940	Per Cent	1956	Per Cent	1960	Per Cent	1964	Per Cent
USSR	153.0	100.0	587.7	100.0	806.1	100.0	1,086.8	100.0
RSFSR[b]	112.7	73.7	354.1	60.2	490.5	60.9	733.7	67.5
Northwest	28.6	18.7	113.7	19.3	137.9	17.1	158.1	14.6
European North	1.4	0.9	6.7	1.1	9.5	1.2	9.3	.9
Centre	24.1	15.8	61.4[c]	10.5	79.4	9.9	194.3	17.9
Volga-W. Urals	34.2	22.4	74.9[c]	12.7	93.6	11.6	105.0	9.7
Black Earth	6.2	4.0	20.1[c]	3.4	25.0	3.1	28.8	2.6
S. Volga	-13.2	8.6	30.7	5.2	39.8	4.9	93.8	8.6
Urals	3.7	2.4	14.6	2.5	18.1	2.3	20.6	1.9
C. Siberia			.9	.2	3.4	.4	11.3	1.0
Far East			22.8	3.9	29.5	3.7	44.6	4.1
N. Caucasus					23.5	2.9	33.0	3.0
Southwest	20.6	13.5	154.2[f]	26.2	213.8	26.5	233.8[d]	21.5
West[c]	18.0	11.8	80.5[g]	13.7	121.8	15.1	139.3[e]	12.8
Caucasus	.4	.3	.6[h]	.2	2.8	.3	5.1	.5
Central Asia	1.2	.8	6.6[i]	1.1	8.0	1.0	9.8	.9

[a]Unless noted otherwise, data are from Narodnoye Khozyaystvo RSFSR v 1958 godu, p. 125; Promyshlennost' RSFSR, p. 187; Narodnoye Khozyaystvo RSFSR v 1964 godu, p. 103; Promyshlennost' SSSR, p. 306; Narodnoye Khozyaystvo RSFSR v 1965 godu, p. 121.

[b]1,300 tons are unaccounted for in the RSFSR in 1940.

[c]The West includes Kaliningrad, Pskov, and Smolensk oblasts of the RSFSR.

[d]Narodnoye Gospodarstvo Ukrainskoy RSR v 1964 rotsi, p. 97.

[e]Largely derived from Itogi Vypolneniya Narodnokhozyaystvennogo Plana SSSR i Soyuznykh Respublik v 1964 godu, pp. 56, 133, 239.

[f]Narodnoye Gospodarstvo Ukrainskoy RSR v 1960 rotsi, p. 80.

[g]Derived from Narodnoye Khozyaystvo Estonskoy SSR, p. 50; Narodnoye Khozyaystvo Latviyskoy SSR, p. 40; Promyshlennost' SSSR, p. 306.

[h]Derived from Promyshlennost' SSSR, p. 306.

[i]Ibid.

32

tive importance by 1964, while the two major regions of paperboard production outside the RSFSR—the Southwest and West—
despite significant fluctuations in intervening years, have increased in relative production since 1940 (Table 7). Paperboard production is located in the central and western parts of
the European USSR to a far greater degree than either lumber
or paper production. Those regions with adequate supplies of
roundwood which account for considerable production of paper
in 1964, or increases in paper production since 1940—the Urals,
Central Siberia, and the Far East—produce only 7 per cent of
Soviet paperboard. This is less than the production of the
Southern Volga region alone. The European North is of almost
no consequence—equal in importance with production in Central Asia. In fact, except for the minor increase in the share
of Central Siberia and the Far East, growth of paperboard production in the USSR since 1940 has occurred primarily in regions near to the industrial consumers of paperboard—in the
Centre and Southern Volga regions, and to a lesser extent, in
the Southwest and West. This means, however, that growth
has chiefly occurred in regions which are in the western, central, or southern European parts of the country, away from the
location of the forest resource. Perhaps this phenomenon is
accounted for by the very small weight-loss in converting
roundwood into paperboard whereas the weight-loss in all other
branches of the wood-processing industry is much greater.

REGIONAL DISTRIBUTION AND STRUCTURE
OF CONTEMPORARY SOVIET WOOD-PROCESSING

Use of the term, roundwood equivalent, assumes that roundwood is the only wood raw material requirement. Consumption
of reeds, straw, and cotton stems in production of pulp is almost insignificant in the USSR.[15] Waste paper is important as

---

[15]Personal communication from Mr. J. Holowacz, April 22, 1968.

TABLE 8. PER CENT COMPOSITION OF WOOD-PROCESSING,
BY REGION, BASED ON ROUNDWOOD REQUIREMENTS, 1964.

Regions	Lumber	Plywood	Chemical Pulp	Ground-wood Pulp	Matches	Sleepers	Total	Per Cent of USSR Total Production of These Items
USSR	83.0	2.5	7.0	1.4	.4	5.7	100.0	100.0
RSFSR	81.6	2.1	7.8	1.3	.3	6.9	100.0	82.7
Northwest	68.4	3.5	22.2	1.4	.2	4.3	100.0	8.0
European North	78.0	1.4	15.4	1.2		4.0	100.0	10.1
Centre	89.9	4.9	1.4		.7	3.1	100.0	8.1
Volga-W. Urals	88.5	3.8	4.4	2.6	.7		100.0	10.7
Black Earth	93.1	4.2			2.7		100.0	1.9
S. Volga	100.0						100.0	3.4
Urals	76.1	2.3	8.9	3.3	.1	9.3	100.0	12.5
W. Siberia	87.2	.6			1.3	10.9	100.0	4.0
C. Siberia	82.5	.2	1.2	.2		15.9	100.0	15.2
Far East	72.1	1.1	10.7	1.5	.3	14.3	100.0	4.9
Siberian North	100.0						100.0	.6
N. Caucasus	97.8	2.2					100.0	1.7
Southwest	94.7	2.8	1.2	1.3			100.0	7.7
West	71.5	8.1	15.4	3.4	1.6		100.0	7.1
Caucasus	91.7	1.5	4.1	2.5	.2		100.0	1.0
Central Asia	100.0						100.0	3.0

NOTE: Figures have been rounded to one decimal place. The West includes Kaliningrad, Pskov, and Smolensk oblasts of the RSFSR.

a raw material but is under-utilized by Soviet planners.[16] Obviously, waste from other branches of the wood-processing industry also could be substituted for roundwood. It must be pointed out, however, that by its own admission, the Soviet forest industry is extremely tardy in utilizing the waste chips, slabs, etc., from one process in another process. Therefore, despite consumption of waste paper in production of some chemical pulp, 1964 production totals expressed in roundwood equivalent probably contain an insignificant amount of double counting.

The component distribution of Soviet wood-processing has not previously been measured in terms of a common denominator (roundwood equivalent $[M^3(r)]$, a theoretical unit of measurement) for all oblasts, krays, and autonomous republics in any available source. The magnitude of production of each industry as a percentage of all production in each large regional unit is shown in Table 8 and Figure 4.

Table 8 shows the predominance of lumber production in the regional composition of Soviet primary wood-processing. In all 16 regions, lumber accounts for over two-thirds of regional production while in half of the regions, lumber accounts for at least nine-tenths of regional output. The low share in all but a few cases, of all other forms of wood-processing, except lumber, testifies to the very narrow range of primary output in the Soviet wood-processing industry and suggests that in all Soviet regions, most of the primary conversion of roundwood involves a low-value product which has undergone very little processing.

[16]Waste paper in 1967 served as the raw material for production of 18 per cent of the Soviet Union's paper output. Paper produced on the basis of waste paper is used chiefly in the manufacture of cardboard. In 1967, 1,234,000 tons of waste paper were consumed as raw material in the paper industry. B. P. Osanov, laboratory head of the USSR Central Paper Research Institute has recently criticized heavily the Soviet attitude toward waste paper as one in which "no real attention is paid to scrap paper as a raw material source, and the collection of waste paper is conducted on a level approaching that of children's play" (quoted in "Put Out the Bonfire," Current Abstracts of the Soviet Press, I, No. 1 [1968], p. 7). Furthermore, the use of paper regenerated from waste paper in the manufacture of cardboard is itself wasted as scrap paper, contains from 15-40 per cent cellulose, and could be used in the manufacture of newsprint and bookpaper (ibid.).

TABLE 9. DISTRIBUTION OF PULP, PAPER, AND PAPERBOARD PRODUCTION, 1964

Regions	Chemical Pulp[a] Tons x 10³	Per Cent	Groundwood Pulp[b] Tons x 10³	Per Cent	Total Pulp Per Cent	Paper[c] Tons x 10³	Per Cent	Paperboard[d] Tons x 10³	Per Cent	Total Paper and Paper-board, %
USSR	2,933.0	100.0	1,150.0	100.0	100.0	3,033.2	100.0	1,086.8	100.0	100.0
RSFSR	2,696.0	91.9	846.4	73.6	88.6	2,471.0	81.5	733.7	67.5	79.3
Northwest	746.1	25.4	92.0	8.0	22.5	707.9	23.3	158.1	14.6	22.0
European North	657.1	22.4	95.4	8.3	20.1	190.9	6.3	9.3	.9	5.5
Centre	49.1	1.6			1.4	120.4	4.0	194.3	17.9	6.1
Volga-W. Urals	199.7	6.8	321.2	20.1	9.0	332.3	11.0	105.0	9.7	10.8
Black Earth						40.6	1.3	28.8	2.6	1.5
S. Volga						51.0	1.7	93.8	8.6	2.7
Urals	468.2	16.0	340.4	29.6	18.2	596.3	19.6	20.6	1.9	17.0
W. Siberia						1.9	.1			.05
C. Siberia	78.0	2.7	25.3	2.2	2.6	88.2	2.9	11.3	1.0	2.6
Far East	220.6	7.5	62.1	5.4	7.2	215.0	7.1	44.6	4.1	6.6
N. Caucasus								33.0	3.0	.5
Southwest	38.3	1.3	82.8	7.2	2.3	174.6	5.8	233.8	21.5	8.1
West*	458.8	15.6	200.1	17.4	15.9	466.2	15.3	139.3	12.8	15.0
Caucasus	17.1	.6	20.7	1.8	.8	36.4	1.2	5.1	.5	1.1
Central Asia						11.5	.4	9.8	.9	.5

*The West includes Kaliningrad, Pskov, and Smolensk oblasts of the RSFSR.

[a]Figures for 1964 production within the RSFSR are estimates made from 1960 figures, for which an oblast breakdown is obtainable. Data for 1960 are from Promyshlennost' SSSR, p. 302; Promyshlennost' RSFSR, p. 183. Except for oblasts where known increases in production had occurred, the RSFSR growth increment 1960-1964 was allocated in proportion to 1960 production. Estimates were based on Narodnoye Khozyaystvo SSSR v 1964 godu, pp. 133, 236; RSFSR v Tsifrakh v 1965 godu, p. 44. Yarmola, Voprosy Lesosnabzheniya, p. 238. Production data for major union republics were obtained from Narodnoye Gospodarstvo Ukrainskoy RSR v 1964 rotsi, p. 97; Itogi Vypolneniya Narodnokhozyaystvennogo Plana SSSR i Soyuznykh Respublik v 1964 godu, pp. 133, 168, 239.

[b]The regional roundwood requirement for groundwood pulp was estimated from Yarmola, Voprosy Lesosnabzheniya, p. 238. Using conversion factors, the roundwood requirement was converted into physical output units for 1964. Production was allocated to oblast units on the basis of statements found in a variety of secondary sources. USSR production figure is for 1963 (Promyshlennost' SSSR, p. 302).

[c]See footnotes to Table 4.

[d]See footnotes to Table 4.

36

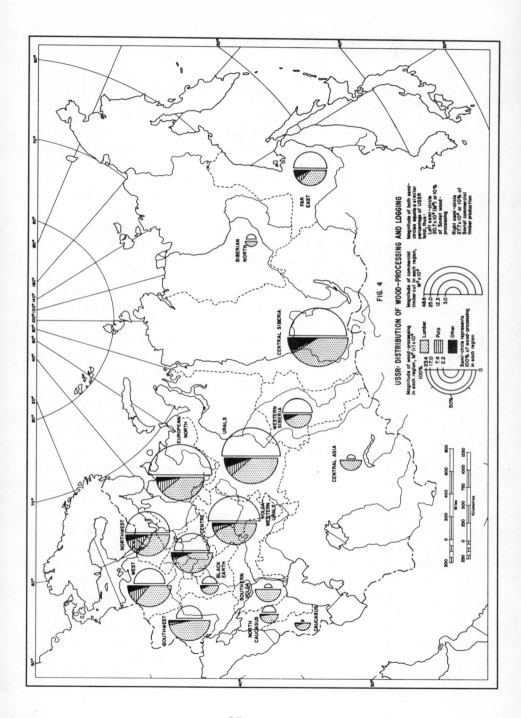

USSR: DISTRIBUTION OF WOOD-PROCESSING AND LOGGING

FIG. 4

Magnitude of both semi-
circles equals a similar
percentage of USSR
total; thus:
Left semi-circle
20.7 x 10⁶ (m³) or 10%
of Soviet wood-
processing

Right semi-circle
27.7 x 10⁶ (m³) or 10%
of Soviet commercial
timber production

Magnitude of commercial
timber cut in each region, M³ x10⁶
48.6
25.0
12.3
3.0

Magnitude of wood-processing
in each region, M³ (r) x10⁶
23.4
17.0
7.4
2.2

Lumber
Pulp
Other

Semi-circle represents
100% of wood-processing
in each region

50%   100%

CONTEMPORARY DISTRIBUTION
OF PULP PRODUCTION

Production of pulp, the chief raw material for production of
paper and paperboard, is concentrated in four regions, three
of which are in the RSFSR (Table 9). Most production of pulp
occurs in regions with adequate forest resources, the only ex-
ception of any significance being production in the West. Production is concentrated in resource areas which are on the
immediate periphery of the European market. Production in
the West, a forest deficient area, can largely be attributed to
the complex political history of the area and the impact of
changes in national boundaries (and, consequently, national
markets) on the economics of production. Similarly, Soviet
production of pulp in the Far East could be termed "acciden-
tal," and would normally not be expected to be as developed;
large, unexploited forests lie between the European concentration of population (the market) and the Far East. Under normal
economic and political conditions, the forests of Central Siberia
would be expected to act as an intervening opportunity to eastward expansion in the pulp industry. Unlike the lumber, paper,
and paperboard industries, production of pulp is almost entirely absent from central European Russia and Central Asia.

In Table 9, production of groundwood and chemical pulp
has been expressed as a total figure for all pulp production in
terms of roundwood equivalent. Production figures in similar
terms have been calculated for paper and paperboard. These
figures, in terms of roundwood equivalent, have been expressed
in each case as a percentage of total USSR production. Contrast
of the percentage distribution of all pulp with the total for paper
and paperboard, for each region, provides an approximate estimate of the degree to which all pulp production is co-located
with production of paper and paperboard. The coefficient of
geographic association between the location of total pulp production and total paper and paperboard production is .82, suggesting a moderately strong spatial association. There is a
very close correspondence in the relative share of each aggregate production figure found in the Northwest, Volga-Western
Urals, Urals, and the West. These four regions produce 65.6
per cent of the total pulp and 64.8 per cent of the total paper
and paperboard. Only one region, the European North, producing approximately four times more pulp than paper and

paperboard, appears to be completely atypical of the general pattern of spatial association. Perhaps this deviation reflects a regional concentration of production of pulp, destined for internal and foreign markets, to facilitate both scale economies in utilization of equipment, and lower costs of interregional roundwood shipments.

The close spatial correspondence between production of pulp and production of paper and paperboard suggests that plants in the pulp-deficient regions of the Centre, Black Earth, Southern Volga, Western Siberia, the North Caucasus, and Central Asia are supplied with surplus pulp from the major regions of pulp production. Supply of such plants with pulp produced in other regions probably reflects the economies of scale of pulp production, both in the sense that pulp plants must produce a specific minimum output for production to be profitable, and in the sense that even if total pulp requirements at plants in pulp-deficient regions are significant, these plants may need several différent kinds of pulp. Shipment of pulp rather than roundwood to the various pulp-deficient regions also reflects the differences in weight-loss ratios between conversion of roundwood to pulp and pulp to paper or paperboard.

III

The Forest Resource

The location of the chief raw material—roundwood—of the Soviet wood-processing industry can be thought of as the location of the forest, or the location of logging activity. In fact, the two are inseparable. The location of logging activity is important to present raw material assembly, while the location of the general reserve of timber is important for assessing past and future changes in the regional distribution of logging and the wood-processing industry.

MEASUREMENT AND DATA

Soviet forests are allocated to three main official organizations: (1) central forestry organs (and Regional Economic Councils [Sovnarkhozy] between 1957 and 1965), (2) central non-forestry ministries and departments, and (3) collective farms. From 1957 to 1965, 95 per cent of the forested area was managed by central state forestry organs and by the Sovnarkhozy. Of the total forested area, the Sovnarkhozy managed 86.5 per cent, while agencies of forest administration and union republic ministries of forest economy and forest industry managed 8.5 per cent; various other non-forest central ministries and central departments managed 2.1 per cent of the forested area; col-

lective farms managed 2.9 per cent.[1] The forests of greatest
importance to the forest industry as a whole were those con-
trolled by the Sovnarkhozy. When the Ministry of Timber,
Wood-working, Pulp, and Paper was formed in 1965, forests
previously allocated to the Sovnarkhozy were taken over by it.
By a decree of the Presidium of the Supreme Soviet of the
USSR on June 11, 1968, this ministry was divided into the
USSR Ministry of Timber and Wood-Processing, and the USSR
Ministry of Pulp and Paper.

Wood moves into processing centres from all three groups
of organizations which control the forest resource. Although
most wood since 1965 appears to come from the centralized
ministries, the reserves controlled by all organizations are
included in the figures of Forested Area and Actual Growing
Stock used here. These data are for January 1, 1961.

Forests controlled by all agencies can be broken down into
the following categories. Within the total area of the forest reserve lands (obschaya ploshchad'), the area of forest reserve
is categorized by (1) forest area (lesnaya ploshchad') including
(a) forested area (pokrytaya lesom), (b) immature forest—
crowns are not closed—(nesomknyvshiyesya lesokul'tury), (c)
forest land which does not support timber—but land suitable
for producing timber—(nepokrytaya lesom), and (2) unforested
land (nelesnaya ploshchad')—water, pasture, land occupied by
buildings, roads, swamps, etc. The unit of measurement used
in this study is forested area (pokrytaya lesom).[2]

The distribution of forest reserves is measured by the term,
Actual Growing Stock (obshchiy zapas nasazhdeniy) which is expressed in M^3. This unit is broken down into various age groups:
juvenile (molodnyaki), average age (srednevozrastnye), approaching maturity (prispevayushchiye), and mature (spelye).
The average density of growing timber per hectare is based on
the amount of Actual Growing Stock of principal species. This
yields volume per unit area.

The rate of growth of the forests in any oblast, kray, or
autonomous republic (ASSR) is measured by the Mean Annual
Increment per hectare of principal species. This unit of meas-

---

[1] D. T. Kovalin, ed., Spravochnik Lesnichego, p. 623.

[2] All Russian terms described are from Kovalin, Spravochnik Lesnichego, pp. 623, 626,
and P. V. Vasil'yev, "USSR Forest Resources and Features of their Inventory," Unasylva,
XV, No. 3 (1961), 119-124.

urement, in M^3 per hectare, reflects the total volume of standing timber and the age of the principal species.

Figures for Annual Allowable Cut are presented in Soviet statistics for Official Economic Regions until 1960 but not by oblast, kray, or ASSR. After 1960, no such figures for the USSR have been published. Official Soviet figures of Annual Allowable Cut apply to the State Forest Reserve and do not include the forests under the jurisdiction of non-forest central organs or the collective farms. Thus, even if current estimates of Annual Allowable Cut were published, they would have to be adjusted to include cutting in forests beyond the jurisdiction of either the Ministry of Timber and Wood-Processing or the Ministry of Pulp and Paper.

The official total Soviet Annual Allowable Cut for 1959 can be closely approximated by multiplying the average national Mean Annual Increment per hectare by the total forested area. Using this technique, the Annual Allowable Cut was calculated for major Soviet regions for 1959 and compared with the official Annual Allowable Cut for the forests under the jurisdiction of the central forest agencies and the Sovnarkhozy. Although the Annual Allowable Cut and the Mean Annual Increment are almost identical for the USSR as a whole, they do vary considerably in individual regions. Official policy appears to allow for overcutting in northern and eastern regions and discourages more than partial cutting of forests in most central, western, and southern regions. Despite the effect of such planning policy, the technique used to derive Annual Allowable Cut from rates of Mean Annual Increment per hectare appears to have validity in establishing a crude limit for estimating the upper limit of timber cutting on a sustained yield basis. In Table 10, the Annual Allowable Cut has been calculated from Mean Annual Increment per hectare for regions used in this study. It should be noted that the figures for Actual Cut include fuelwood.

The material presented in Table 10 suggests that overcutting is now occurring only in the Northwest while cutting in all other regions, except the European North and the Volga-Western Urals, is well below the Mean Annual Increment. It is probable that the Annual Allowable Cut for most regions is too high, as the figures in Table 10 undoubtedly include forests which would not be cut in any country—parks, government range lands, military establishments, etc. In addition, the estimates do not take into account the age of species, the economics of logging,

TABLE 10. CALCULATION OF ANNUAL ALLOWABLE CUT
ON THE BASIS OF MEAN ANNUAL INCREMENT, 1964 (M^3 x 10^3)

Regions	(1) Mean Annual Increment	(2) Actual Cut (Including Fuelwood)	(3) (1) - (2)	(4) (2) as Per Cent of (1)
USSR	985,936	385,292	600,644	39.0
RSFSR	903,129	352,708	550,421	39.0
Northwest	26,490	32,773	-6,283	124.0
European North	60,604	59,699	905	98.5
Centre	41,985	28,018	13,967	66.7
Volga-W. Urals	51,196	48,135	3,061	94.0
Black Earth	10,570	4,559	6,011	43.1
S. Volga	5,558	1,996	3,562	35.9
Urals	93,123	66,107	27,016	70.9
W. Siberia	52,503	16,885	35,618	32.1
C. Siberia	317,112	61,795	255,317	19.4
Far East	101,196	19,192	˙82,004	18.9
Siberian North	126,324	4,916	121,408	3.8
N. Caucasus	8,693	4,648	4,045	53.4
Southwest	22,971	12,149	10,822	52.8
West	36,066	20,949	15,117	58.0
Caucasus	7,121	1,338	5,783	18.7
Central Asia	24,424	2,133	22,291	8.7

SOURCE: Mean Annual Increment per hectare and Forested Area were obtained or derived from Kovalin, Spravochnik Lesnichego, pp. 626-654.

Actual Cut was obtained from Narodnoye Khozyaystvo SSSR v 1964 godu, p. 197, and
Narodnoye Khozyaystvo RSFSR v 1964 godu, pp. 95-96.

or the suitability of stands for satisfying demands for commercial timber of suitable specifications. This is probably especially true in Central Asia, the West, Southwest, Black
Earth, and Southern Volga regions. Nevertheless, Table 10
does provide a statement about the theoretical regional upper
limits to annual cutting.

Piecemeal statistics are available in most Soviet articles
and books dealing with the forest resource in the USSR. Reliable and current data for every oblast, kray, or ASSR are not
as widely publicized. For each section of the present chapter,
however, there are recent Soviet sources which provide comprehensive data.[3] Data presented in Table 14 (Stumpage Fees)
and in Table 15 (Actual Production Costs of Marketable Roundwood) are less reliable in some respects than data presented in

[3]Kovalin, Spravochnik Lesnichego, pp. 623-663; Gorovoy, "Lesnye Resursy SSSR i ikh
Ispol'zovaniye, " in Zemel'nye Resursy i Lesnye Resursy SSSR, p. 111; A. D. Ponomarev,
"Lesnoy Fond SSSR, " Lesnoye Khozyaystvo, XVI, No. 6 (1963), 48-55; V. P. Tseplyaev,
Lesnoye Khozyaystvo SSSR.

other tables throughout the study. In Tables 14 and 15, the type of roundwood is unspecified. Average stumpage fees and actual production costs for each region within the RSFSR vary in reliability depending on the number of observations used to calculate regional averages from the original source. The original source presented data for various oblasts, krays, and autonomous republics within a different regional framework.

THE FOREST

Nearly all the forest resource is located within the Russian republic. Whether measured in terms of area or volume, only the resource of the RSFSR is of any importance to the Soviet forest industry as a whole. It is clear from Table 11 that both criteria—total forested area and actual growing stock—are very close in magnitude from region to region, with minor variation shown for only Central Siberia, the Far East, and the Siberian

TABLE 11. DISTRIBUTION OF THE SOVIET FOREST RESOURCE 1961

Regions	Total Forest Area[a]		Actual Growing Stock[b]	
	Ha. x 10³	Per Cent	M³ x 10⁶	Per Cent
USSR	738,787.5	100.0	80,215.51	100.0
RSFSR	696,129.2	94.2	77,591.78	96.7
Northwest	19,475.8	2.6	1,925.10	2.4
European North	56,989.7	7.7	6,006.68	7.5
Centre	14,403.9	2.0	1,479.05	1.8
Volga-W. Urals	20,962.9	2.8	2,381.69	2.9
Black Earth	3,293.8	.4	294.60	.4
S. Volga	2,098.9	.3	143.61	.2
Urals	69,230.1	9.4	8,063.10	10.0
W. Siberia	31,760.2	4.3	3,962.04	4.9
C. Siberia	222,948.1	30.2	29,022.47	36.2
Far East	80,281.3	10.9	10,283.12	12.8
Siberian North	168,311.7	22.8	13,281.71	16.6
N. Caucasus	3,339.8	.4	533.42	.7
Southwest	7,486.4	1.0	768.83	1.0
West[c]	14,920.3	2.0	1,196.70	1.5
Caucasus	3,764.3	.5	530.24	.7
Central Asia	19,520.3	2.7	343.15	.4

[a]Kovalin, Spravochnik Lesnichego, pp. 628-649.

[b]Ibid.

[c]The West includes Kaliningrad, Pskov, and Smolensk oblasts of the RSFSR.

44

North. It can be seen as well that the European North, the Urals, Western and Central Siberia, the Far East, and the Siberian North account for 88 per cent of the volume of Soviet reserves. The magnitude of the reserves in these regions, however, when viewed from the standpoint of accessibility, takes on a different perspective (Figure 5). Only the European North, the Urals, and parts of Western Siberia are within easy range of the market for wood products.[4] These three regions account for only 22.4 per cent of the total volume of reserves. Although cutting occurs in Central Siberia, the Siberian North, and the Far East (which account for 65.6 per cent of the volume of reserves), the relative inaccessibility of these areas suggests that other measures may have to be considered before concluding that the logical path of expansion of logging in the Soviet Union is eastward.

Another factor besides distance which reduces the economic potential of eastern forests under current technology, is the predominance of larch in Soviet, and especially in Siberian, forests. Table 12 shows the relative importance of the major commercial species of wood in both the USSR and the RSFSR.

In order to exploit the forests (1) north and east of the Angara-Yenisey confluence in Krasnoyarsk Kray and Irkutsk oblast, (2) in the southern and central portions of the Siberian North, and (3) in most of Amur oblast and Khabarovsk kray, Soviet foresters will have to develop ways of utilizing larch. At the present time, utilization of this wood, except as lumber, is not technically feasible. In addition, transportation of the wood in round form is hampered by its density and propensity to sink.

The major stands of pine in the RSFSR are found in the Northwest (especially in Karelia ASSR and Murmansk oblast), in the European North throughout the Pechora River basin, in the northeastern Urals and Tyumen oblast, and in the Angara basin of Central Siberia. The reserves west of, and including, the Urals appear to be of greater potential economic significance than pine reserves east of the Urals, due to the proximity of the former to domestic and foreign European markets.

The main concentration of spruce is in the European North, the Volga-Western Urals, the western Urals, Khabarovsk kray east of the Amur river, and in central Sakhalin oblast. The stands of spruce have a much better location than those of pine

4Distribution of forests in the USSR is portrayed well in Atlas SSSR, pp. 90-91.

45

TABLE 12. PRIMARY COMMERCIAL TIMBER SPECIES

	USSR $M^3 \times 10^6$	Per Cent	RSFSR $M^3 \times 10^6$	Per Cent
Pine	14,764.69	19.3	14,162.35	19.1
Spruce	12,682.56	16.6	12,315.73	16.6
Fir	2,343.42	3.1	2,148.05	2.9
Larch	28,276.33	37.0	28,240.07	38.0
Siberian Stone Pine (Kedr)	5,992.68	7.8	5,987.15	8.1
Birch	6,533.26	8.6	6,371.19	8.6
Other	5,751.67	7.6	4,902.34	6.7
TOTAL—all wood and shrub species under the jurisdiction of the Ministry of Timber, Wood-Working, Pulp and Paper	76,344.61	100.0	74,126.88	100.0

SOURCE: Kovalin, Spravochnik Lesnichego, p. 650.

because they are closer either to the European markets or to the Pacific littoral with its possibilities for export.

From Table 12 it is clear that Soviet reserves of fir are rather limited. They are concentrated in Kemerovo oblast and in southern Krasnoyarsk kray and from these areas the chief route to the market is by rail over the trunk Siberian railways. Spruce and fir appear together in several noticeable small concentrations in the southeast of the Maritime kray, in the southeast of Tomsk oblast, southwest Chita oblast, central Bashkiria, and to the west of Komsomol'sk on the lower Amur.

The Siberian Stone Pine (kedr) is not characterized by large concentrations. Apart from the limited predominance in southwest Irkutsk oblast, in the Tuva ASSR and in the Maritime kray, the Siberian Stone Pine (kedr) is found scattered throughout the eastern regions of the Soviet Union south of 60° latitude and east of the Ob' river.

The volume of birch in the USSR is approximately the same as that of Siberian Stone Pine, but the characteristics of its distribution are somewhat different. Although both species are found in the central portion of Western Siberia and Krasnoyarsk kray, the forests of the Ob'-Irtysh interfluve consist almost entirely of birch, while the two species, birch and Siberian Stone Pine (kedr), together comprise the forests on the east bank of the Yenisey river between its confluence with the Angara and the river Nizhnaya Tunguska. Birch is found in large amounts in southern Kamchatka oblast (Stone Birch) and throughout the mixed and broadleaved forests of central European Russia.

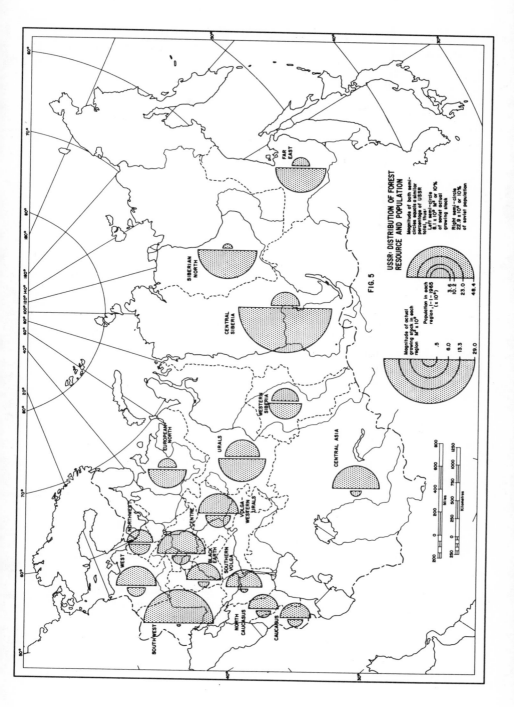

FIG. 5

USSR: DISTRIBUTION OF FOREST RESOURCE AND POPULATION

Each of the species discussed above has its own commercial significance in the Soviet Union.[5] Most coniferous lumber is cut from pine (Scots) and Siberian Stone Pine (Kedr), while hardwood lumber is cut from a variety of species such as oak and birch. In decreasing order of importance, spruce, fir and pine are the principal species used for the production of wood pulp. Birch, a small proportion of aspen and some softwood are the species used for production of plywood. Poles and railway sleepers are derived chiefly from Siberian Larch and Scots Pine. Pit props, however, come from a wide variety of species such as pine, spruce, larch, Siberian Stone Pine (kedr) and fir. Birch in split form is often used for shutes, side supports, flooring, etc., within mines.

FOREST VOLUME AND
RATES OF GROWTH

Consideration of the distribution of forest resources and evaluation of trends in the utilization of forests must be tempered not only by consideration of the differences in the total volume of the resource and its accessibility from region to region, but also by differences in volume per hectare and rates of growth. The economic significance of any forest depends not only on its age and accessibility, but also on the density of timber (volume per hectare) and rates of growth of the principal species. The rate of growth of any forest is important to the volume of Annual Allowable Cut and to the time required for a seedling to grow into mature timber. Table 13 shows that the regions of the central and southern European USSR have the highest rates of Mean Annual Increment per hectare, although they account for very little of the Actual Growing Stock. While it is unrealistic to expect the Soviet Union to allocate good agricultural land in these regions to the production of trees, it is still possible that careful forest management within these areas on soils unsuitable to mechanized agriculture could, in the long run, be of greater benefit to the national economy than the exploitation of less productive forests in zones on the periphery of the economic ecumene.

[5]Information provided by Mr. J. Holowacz in a personal communication to the author, March 11, 1968.

TABLE 13. VARIATIONS IN VOLUME AND RATE OF GROWTH
OF PRINCIPAL FOREST SPECIES IN SELECTED REGIONS, 1961[a]

Regions	Average Volume of Principal Species Hectare[b] M^3	Mean Annual Increment of Principal Species Hectare[c] M^3
USSR	121	1.3
RSFSR	120	1.3
Karelia ASSR	121	1.1
Komi ASSR	99	.9
Kaluga oblast	121	3.5
Mari ASSR	120	2.6
Bryansk oblast	114	3.4
Volgograd oblast	69	2.9
Sverdlovsk oblast	136	1.8
Tomsk oblast	145	1.5
Buryat ASSR	131	1.2
Amur oblast	114	1.2
Yakut ASSR	94	.8
Stavropol kray	140	2.3
Ukraine	127	3.1
Latvia	108	2.3
Byelorussia	80	2.4
Azerbaydzhan	136	1.7
Uzbekistan[d]	69	.6

[a]Forests under the jurisdiction of collective farms, non-forest ministries, trusts, park boards, etc., are excluded from this table.
[b]Kovalin, Spravochnik Lesnichego, pp. 653-654.
[c]Ibid.
[d]Excluding Haloxylon.

The figures presented in Table 13 for average volume per hectare and Mean Annual Increment reflect the age and type of principal species, and the physical and climatic conditions prevalent in each region. Thus, for example, physical and climatic conditions in the Southern Volga region favour a high rate of growth of deciduous species. Species in most stands in this region are juvenile or approaching maturity, thus being characterized by greater rates of growth but a lower average volume per hectare than would be found in a region of similar species having mature or average timber.

Central Siberia and the Far East, on the other hand, where most stands are completely mature, are characterized by a relatively low Mean Annual Increment per hectare (rate of growth) but a substantial average volume per hectare. This signifies a substantial amount of standing timber but a low an-

49

nual increment due to the age of the stand. Much the same sort of relationship prevails in the Siberian North where most stands are completely mature. Different physical and climatic conditions, however, result in a lower absolute rate of growth and a smaller volume per hectare. [6]

Growth rates in the European North, the Urals, Western and Central Siberia, the Far East, and the Siberian North, which together account for 88 per cent of the volume of Soviet reserves, are roughly one-half to one-third of those in the Centre, Volga-Western Urals, Black Earth, and Southern Volga Regions. Soviet officials must balance the relative costs of reforestation and the time needed by a new forest to reach maturity against capital costs, alternate land uses, and markets in each area before any real assessment can be made of the potential significance of the great peripheral forests in the USSR. Regional differences in mean annual increment per hectare and, to a lesser degree, average volume per hectare, dispel any rash enthusiasm for imprudent utilization of northern and eastern forests.

LOGGING

Economic Stimuli
Governments traditionally place a value on a tree, known as a "stumpage fee," and the user must assess whether the cost of producing and marketing roundwood from that tree justifies paying the tax. Stumpage fees in the Soviet Union should render some clue as to the relative priorities the state has placed on utilizing forests in various regions. Assuming that pine, spruce, and fir are the major species in demand, and that the costs of harvesting 1 M^3 of any species is more or less equivalent within any region (although specific costs vary from lot to lot), it is reasonable to expect Soviet stumpage fees to indicate the regions where intensive cutting is officially encouraged. [7] The level of Soviet stumpage fees is supposed to take into account regional characteristics of the nature of the timber stands, type of wood (commercial or fuel wood), size of the

[6]Derived from Kovalin, Spravochnik Lesnichego, pp. 626-652.

[7]V. P. Tseplyaev, Lesnoye Khozyaystvo SSSR, p. 32. Tseplyaev gives a good account of changes in understanding and application of stumpage fees in the USSR in Soviet times, as well as reasons for introduction of a new schedule of fees in 1966 (pp. 30-32).

TABLE 14. STUMPAGE FEES INCURRED
IN THE PRODUCTION OF 1 M³ OF UN-
SPECIFIED COMMERCIAL ROUNDWOOD,
1961 (Regional Averages)

Regions	Rubles
USSR	0.43
RSFSR	0.33
Northwest	0.51
European North	0.27
Centre	0.51
Volga-W. Urals	0.58
Black Earth	N. A.
S. Volga	N. A.
Urals	0.36
W. Siberia	0.29
C. Siberia	0.29
Far East	0.26
Siberian North	0.22
N. Caucasus	N. A.
Southwest	1.76
West	0.63
Caucasus	1.90
Central Asia	0.23

SOURCE: Vasil'yev and Zheludkov, "Problemy Uluchsheniya Otraslevoy Struktury i
Razmeshcheniya Lesnoy Promyshlennosti, "
pp. 405-406.

tree, length of rail and water hauls to the market, and general
features of the various forest-economic zones. [8]

The general stumpage prices shown in Table 14 display a
noticeable decline away from the southern and central European parts of the USSR, where they are highest, and they reach
a minimum level in the Siberian North. All regions identified
previously as containing most of the volume of Actual Growing
Stock have very low stumpage fees. In addition, it is possible
to distinguish relative differences in the level of the fees as
distance increases away from the central European part of the
USSR. The stumpage prices in Table 14 clearly show that official taxing policy is to encourage cutting in the peripheral
forests, discourage it in the Caucasus, West and Southwest,
and place some restrictions on cutting in the Northwest, Centre, and Volga-Western Urals regions.

[8]P. V. Vasil'yev and A. G. Zheludkov, "Problemy Uluchsheniya Otraslevoy Struktury i
Razmeshcheniya Lesnoy Promyshlennosti, " in Voprosy Razmeshcheniya Proizvodstva v
SSSR, ed. by N. N. Nekrasov, p. 409.

TABLE 15. PRODUCTION COSTS OF 1 M^3
OF COMMERCIAL ROUNDWOOD, 1961
(Regional Averages)

Regions	Rubles
USSR	6.98
RSFSR	6.80
Northwest	7.51
European North	6.83
Centre	6.64
Volga-W. Urals	6.53
Black Earth	N.A.
S. Volga	N.A.
Urals	7.15
W. Siberia	6.41
C. Siberia	6.74
Far East	10.01
Siberian North	7.44
N. Caucasus	N.A.
Southwest	8.29
West	7.25
Caucasus	14.50
Central Asia	15.15

SOURCE: Vasil'yev and Zheludkov, "Problemy Uluchsheniya Otraslevoy Struktury i Razmeshcheniya Lesnoy Promyshlennosti, " p. 402.

Actual production costs (shown in Table 15), do not correspond in areal variation with official stumpage fees. Conclusions drawn from this table lead back to the position taken earlier: there is economic logic to the belief that continued utilization of northern and Siberian forests is not warranted by cheaper production costs. Production costs in these areas are slightly higher than in regions with greater access to the populated areas of the country. The slight range in the variation of general production costs among the major regions of the RSFSR adds strength to the proposition (developed later in this study) that transport costs play a large role in bringing about the location of wood-processing activity. If production costs from region to region are approximately the same, then differences in transport costs appear to take on critical importance in determining which regions should supply the bulk of Soviet timber to various markets.

Economic obstacles to the development of peripheral forests are reflected in the rates of cutting in the forests of the Northwest, European North, Centre, and Volga-Western Urals regions (Table 10). Assuming that the rates of cutting in column 4 of Table 10 are low for these regions, due to the use of annual increment as a measure of allowable cut, the need for a shift to peripheral forests is paramount and better forms of forest management are required in central and northern European regions. If utilization of Mean Annual Increment alone is used as a criterion for measuring the need to relocate the logging industry, the conclusion is immediately drawn that logging should increase in the Urals and Siberia. This is indeed the case, but the increase in cost to the national economy of the USSR resulting from large-scale eastward expansion of logging should be offset by corresponding movements in the consumers of roundwood. Such concomitant movement, according to Soviet reports, would face high development costs of plant and infrastructure in eastern regions.[9]

The regional shifts in production of timber, lumber, chemical pulp, and paper in relation to Actual Growing Stock, and the shifts of lumber, chemical pulp, and paper production in relation to the timber production have been measured in Table 16 using the coefficient of geographic association.[10] The table shows a trend toward increasing spatial association of both timber production and wood-processing with Actual Growing Stock in the period 1940-1964. On the other hand, production of chemical pulp and paper shows approximately the same spatial association with timber in 1964 as in 1940, while lumber production shows less of a spatial correlation with timber production in 1964 than in 1940. The coefficients suggest that the patterns of distribution of logging and Actual Growing Stock are becoming more similar. Adjustments in the pattern of logging have been matched by concomitant changes in the distribution of chemical pulp and paper production. The pattern of lumber production, however, has become more distinct from that of logging.

The dilemma facing those responsible for making decisions on the future regional distribution of logging in the USSR is paradoxical. Stumpage fees and rates of overcutting clearly en-

---

[9]A good summary of the significance of such statements is contained in Theodore Shabad, "Cost factor now dominant in Soviet resource development program," reprinted from The New York Times in The Globe and Mail, October 31, 1967, p. 8.

[10]Derivation and some of the other uses of the coefficient of geographic association are explained in J. W. Alexander, Economic Geography, pp. 595-597.

TABLE 16. CHANGES IN RAW-MATERIAL ORIENTATION, 1940-1964
(Measured by Coefficients of Geographic Association)

Association of:	1940	1956	1960	1964
Commercial Timber Production: Actual Growing Stock	.51	.53	.53	.57
Lumber Production: Actual Growing Stock	.51	.51	.51	.54
Chemical Pulp Production: Actual Growing Stock	.28	.35	.36	.38
Paper Production: Actual Growing Stock	.28	.35	.36	.38
Lumber Production: Commercial Timber Production	.86	.84	.80	.80
Chemical Pulp Production: Commercial Timber Production	.66	.60	.61	.64
Paper Production: Commercial Timber Production	.65	.66	.65	.66

SOURCES: Commercial timber production: sources listed in Table 17.
Actual Growing Stock: distribution shown in Table 11 for 1961 was used
for all years.
Lumber production: sources listed in Table 5.
Chemical pulp production: data for all years have been derived from
Katsenelenbaum, chief ed., Spravochnik Ekonomista-Bumazhnika, pp. 17-20.
Data for 1955 have been used in place of 1956 data.
Paper production: sources listed in Table 6.
The coefficient, in essence, measures the similarity or difference between the percentage distributions of two phenomena. The coefficients were
derived for 16 regions by (1) obtaining the percentage distribution of each phenomenon throughout the 16 regions, (2) finding the sum of the positive or negative differences between the percent of the phenomena in each region, (3)
subtracting this sum from 100 and (4) converting to an index of 0 to 1.00. If
the percentage distributions of two phenomena are identical, the coefficient
will equal 1.00. The greater the dissimilarity, the closer the coefficient approaches zero. Use of the coefficient of geographic association does not involve the assumption of a normal distribution of the data. In addition, the
coefficient can be calculated for aggregated data, as in Tables 16 and 21.

courage an eastward shift in logging, whereas costs of production
and greater distances from consumers favour maintenance of a
strong logging base in traditional regions with good access to
European markets.

Changes in Regional Location
The Russian republic occupies a paramount position in the production of commercial timber (Table 17). Although this is to be
expected, it is only in recent years that the relative share of
logging has begun to equal the relative share of the volume of
Actual Growing Stock. A noticeable increase, since World War

TABLE 17. DISTRIBUTION OF COMMERCIAL TIMBER PRODUCTION (M³ x 10³)

Regions	1940	Per Cent	1956	Per Cent	1960	Per Cent	1964	Per Cent
USSR	118,246	100.0	222,092	100.0	261,513	100.0	276,874	100.0
RSFSR	101,750	86.0	198,416	89.3	239,340	91.5	255,888	92.4
Northwest	11,119	9.4	19,350	8.7	23,675	9.1	24,911	9.0
European North	18,934	16.0	32,442	14.6	44,590	17.1	47,121	17.0
Centre	8,870	7.5	16,061	7.2	17,568	6.7	16,743	6.0
Volga-W. Urals	14,767	12.5	32,547	14.7	34,995	13.4	132,296	11.7
Black Earth	2,214	1.9	2,316	1.1	2,838	1.1	3,057	1.1
S. Volga	612	.5	1,165	.5	1,153	.4	1,137	.4
Urals	16,535	14.0	35,796	16.1	46,282	17.7	48,319	17.5
W. Siberia	5,614	4.8	10,191	4.6	9,945	3.8	11,467	4.1
C. Siberia	11,877	10.0	31,840	14.3	38,264	14.6	48,644	17.6
Far East	6,190	5.2	10,227	4.6	12,412	4.7	15,236	5.5
Siberian North	2,001	1.7	1,535	.7	2,346	.9	1,881	.7
N. Caucasus	1,506	1.3	2,634	1.2	3,113	1.2	2,834	1.0
Southwest	5,218	4.4	11,554	5.2	10,246	3.9	9,027	3.3
West[a]	11,477	9.7	12,693	5.7	11,977	4.6	12,260	4.4
Caucasus	451	.4	658	.3	863	.3	687	.2
Central Asia	861	.7	1,083	.5	1,246	.5	1,254	.5

SOURCE: Narodnoye Khozyaystvo RSFSR v 1958 godu, pp. 111–113; Narodnoye Khozyaystvo SSSR v 1958 godu, pp. 252–253; Narodnoye Khozyystvo RSFSR v 1964 godu, pp. 90–93; Narodnoye Khozyystvo SSSR v 1964 godu, pp. 194–195.

aThe West includes Kaliningrad, Pskov, and Smolensk oblasts of the RSFSR.

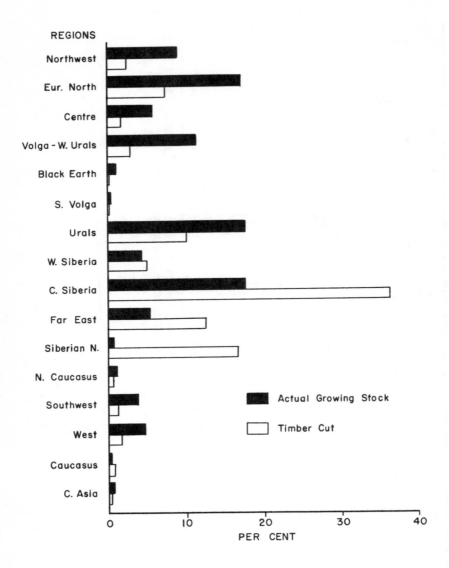

REGIONS

Region	
Northwest	
Eur. North	
Centre	
Volga - W. Urals	
Black Earth	
S. Volga	
Urals	
W. Siberia	
C. Siberia	
Far East	
Siberian N.	
N. Caucasus	
Southwest	
West	
Caucasus	
C. Asia	

■ Actual Growing Stock

□ Timber Cut

PER CENT

Figure 6. Percentage Distribution of Actual
Growing Stock and Commercial Timber Production

II, has been observed in the importance of the Urals and Siberia in national production of timber.

Significant increases in the absolute production of timber after 1940 occurred in all regions except the Black Earth and Siberian North. In recent years, however, production in the Centre, Volga-Western Urals, Southern Volga, North Caucasus, Southwest, West, Caucasus, and Central Asia has levelled off or declined slightly. Only the Northwest, European North, Urals, Western and Central Siberia, and the Far East have shown significant increases in the production of timber. Remarkable increases in production have occurred in Central Siberia, namely, in Krasnoyarsk kray, Irkutsk and Kemerovo oblasts. Relative increases in timber production since 1956, most noticeable in Central Siberia, indicate that in most regions, the same annual volume of timber which was cut in the 1950's is being cut in the 1960's, but that significant further increases in production are occurring primarily in the European North, the Urals, West Siberia, Central Siberia, and the Far East.

Despite growth of timber production in the peripheral forests, a large disproportion still exists between the location of the Actual Growing Stock and the location of logging. In 1964, the coefficient of geographic association between the two activities was .57 (see Fig. 6). Except in those regions where both logging and Actual Growing Stock are less than 1 per cent of the national total, and thus almost insignificant, only Western Siberia has a balanced proportion of logging and Actual Growing Stock. In traditional regions of cutting—the Northwest, European North, Centre, Volga-Western Urals, Southwest, West, and Urals, the relative share of logging far exceeds that of Actual Growing Stock. As noted earlier, except for the European North and the Urals, an increase in logging is not occurring in these regions. In the European North and the Urals, absolute production has increased but the relative share of national timber production of each region has remained almost constant since the late 1950's. Only in Central Siberia, the Far East, and the Siberian North does the relative national share of Actual Growing Stock far exceed the share of timber production.

IV

The Market

The task of estimating precisely the regional consumption of lumber, paper, and other products is beset with difficulties as specific data on consumption are not published in Soviet official handbooks and must be estimated on the basis of population distribution.

An average figure of per capita consumption of lumber was derived for the entire USSR (see note "a, " Table 19). No attempt was made to weight this figure for individual areas by taking into account broad regional differences in per capita utilization of lumber. Consequently, the regional consumption figures calculated for lumber in Table 19 are only crude approximations.

Nearly one-third of the paper consumption in the USSR can be accurately measured, although use of conversion factors is necessary. Consumption of newsprint and typographical paper can be derived from the volume of newspapers, journals, pamphlets, books, etc., published in every oblast, kray, and autonomous republic.[1] The spatial pattern of consumption of other types of paper has been measured on a per capita basis in a manner similar to that used to estimate lumber consumption. Such estimates assume that the distribution of all types of

[1] Pechat' SSSR v 1965 godu, Statisticheskiye Materialy.

TABLE 18. DISTRIBUTION OF POPULATION
(January 1, 1965)

Regions	x 10^3	Per Cent
USSR	229,198	100.0
RSFSR	125,768	54.9
Northwest	7,109	3.1
European North	3,657	1.6
Centre	22,941	10.0
Volga-W. Urals	17,601	7.7
Black Earth	12,020	5.2
S. Volga	13,764	6.0
Urals	13,007	5.7
W. Siberia	7,813	3.4
C. Siberia	10,220	4.5
Far East	4,250	1.9
Siberian North	1,177	.5
N. Caucasus	9,544	4.1
Southwest	48,403	21.1
West	17,661	7.7
Caucasus	11,135	4.9
Central Asia	28,896	12.6

SOURCE: Narodnoye Khozyaystvo SSSR v 1964 godu, pp. 13-17, 18-21.

paper can be measured by assuming uniform consumption per capita throughout the USSR. All estimates of paper consumption appear in Table 20.

ASPECTS OF REGIONAL DEMAND

Population Distribution

The distribution of population (Table 18), which probably closely approximates the spatial pattern of consumption, is significantly different from the distribution of the Actual Growing Stock. Only 17.6 per cent (less than one-fifth) of the Soviet population lives in regions containing the large peripheral forests—the European North, the Urals, all of Siberia, and the Far East— whereas exactly 50 per cent lives in the area comprised by the West, Southwest, Southern Volga, Black Earth, and Centre regions. The large concentrations of population in the Caucasus, North Caucasus, and Central Asia, which together account for 21.6 per cent of the Soviet population, are in marked contrast with the limited forest resources found in these regions. An

TABLE 19. THE DEMAND FOR LUMBER, 1964[a]

Regions	Sawn Lumber M^3 x 10^3
USSR	103,467
RSFSR	56,775
Northwest	3,209
Incl. Leniningrad oblast	2,254
European North	1,651
Centre	10,356
Incl. Moscow oblast	5,287
Volga-W. Urals	7,946
Black Earth	5,426
S. Volga	6,214
Urals	5,872
W. Siberia	3,527
C. Siberia	4,614
Far East	1,918
Siberian North	531
N. Caucasus	4,308
Southwest	21,850
West[b]	7,973
Caucasus	5,027
Central Asia	13,045

[a]The demand for lumber is estimated as per capita consumption:

USSR production:	110,899,000
USSR export:	7,675,600
USSR import:	243,700
Net amount available:	103,467,100
USSR population:	229,198,000

M^3 available per capita: .45143
Consequently, the population in each region is multiplied by .45143.

[b]The West includes Kaliningrad, Pskov, and Smolensk oblasts of the RSFSR.

intermediate position is held by the Northwest and the Volga-Western Urals regions which account for 10.8 per cent of the population. Thus, over seven-tenths of the Soviet population lives in regions which are deficient in supplies of roundwood. The location of areas of population concentration—the market—when coupled with the influence of historical factors and the high cost of developing a sufficient infrastructure in marginal areas, appears to be a significant factor in explaining many of the differences between the spatial location of logging (timber production) and wood-processing (see Fig. 4).

Lumber Demand

Estimates of regional demand for lumber (Table 19) have been calculated on the basis of population distribution. Most of the demand for lumber appears to be outside the roundwood surplus regions, thus necessitating long interregional hauls of timber. The problem to be solved in subsequent analysis is whether production of lumber is cheaper, from the standpoint of transport costs, in northern and eastern regions which have surpluses of roundwood but shortages of local demand, or in western, central, and southern regions which contain most of the Soviet population but very little of either the Actual Growing Stock or logging activity.

Paper Demand

The consumption of newsprint and typographical paper accounts for slightly over one-third of the total market for all paper in the USSR. The consumption of newsprint and typographical paper in the Soviet Union shows a greater localization (Table 20) than any other activity yet measured in this study: a greater concentration than population, processing, or Actual Growing Stock. Centralization of political power, economic administration, and cultural leadership are manifested in the remarkable concentration of Soviet demand (two-thirds) for newsprint and typographical paper in the Centre, primarily in Moscow oblast.

Such a localized market for some forms of paper has several important implications. The location decision for production of newsprint and typographical paper should be a relatively simple matter of choosing (1) a region of sufficient roundwood or a location near to Moscow and (2) several locations which best serve the remaining widely dispersed market. The characteristics of the market should permit significant use to be made of economies of scale in the distribution of plant and equipment. However, the market pattern for other papers, as estimated here, is close to that of lumber and extremely difficult to assess without better data. The decision for the location of production of both "other" papers and lumber appears to be much more complex than for production of newsprint and typographical paper.

Changes in Market Orientation

Coefficients of geographic association have been used to measure the spatial association of lumber, chemical pulp, and paper

TABLE 20. REGIONAL DEMAND FOR NEWSPRINT, TYPOGRAPHICAL
AND OTHER PAPERS, AND ROUNDWOOD EQUIVALENTS, 1964[a]

Regions	Tons of Paper x 10³				Total Consumption* M³(r) x 10³e	Per Cent	Consumption, Other Papers M³(r) x 10³	Per Cent	Total Consumption, All Paper M³(r) x 10³	Per Cent
	News-papers[b]	Books,[c] Pamphlets	Periodicals[d]	Total						
USSR	533.16	352.93	153.48	1,039.57	3,326.64	100.0	6,214.50	100.0	9,541.14	100.0
RSFSR	400.03	280.18	136.54	816.75	2,613.61	78.6	3,411.76	54.9	6,025.37	63.2
Northwest	8.60	12.86	3.04	24.50	78.40	2.4	192.65	3.1	271.05	2.8
Incl. Leningrad oblast	6.10	12.13	3.00	21.23	67.94	2.0	136.70	2.2	204.64	2.2
European North	3.63	.27	.03	3.93	12.58	.4	99.47	1.6	112.05	1.2
Centre	298.82	256.15	131.06	686.03	2,195.30	66.0	621.45	10.0	2,816.75	29.5
Incl. Moscow oblast	288.76	255.30	130.98	675.04	2,160.13	64.9	316.93	5.1	2,477.06	26.0
Volga-W. Urals	17.37	3.18	.68	21.23	67.94	2.0	478.51	7.7	546.45	5.7
Black Earth	10.64	.89	.09	11.62	37.18	1.1	323.15	5.2	360.33	3.8
S. Volga	13.20	1.47	.38	15.05	48.16	1.4	372.87	6.0	421.03	4.4
Urals	11.86	1.44	.53	13.83	44.26	1.3	354.22	5.7	398.48	4.2
W. Siberia	7.34	.89	.34	8.57	27.42	.8	211.29	3.4	238.71	2.5
C. Siberia	9.08	.90	.09	10.07	33.22	1.0	279.65	4.5	311.87	3.3
Far East	6.18	.45	.06	6.69	21.41	.6	118.07	1.9	139.48	1.5
Siberian North	1.87	.21	.05	2.13	6.82	.2	31.07	.5	37.89	.4
N. Caucasus	8.18	1.32	.19	9.69	31.01	.9	254.79	4.1	285.80	3.0
Southwest	57.77	33.25	6.61	97.63	312.42	9.4	1,311.25	21.1	1,623.67	17.0
West[f]	31.47	14.42	4.75	50.64	162.05	4.9	478.52	7.7	640.57	6.7
Caucasus	15.20	10.15	1.36	26.71	85.47	2.6	304.51	4.9	389.98	4.1
Central Asia	31.95	15.08	4.22	51.25	164.00	4.9	783.03	12.6	947.03	9.9

*Total consumption of Newspapers, Books, Pamphlets and Periodicals.

a The annual output of all literature in terms of printers sheets (pechatnyy list ottiski) for each region was converted to tons of paper through use of appropriate conversion factors. The type of paper available for meeting the demand of newspapers, books, pamphlets, and periodicals (termed newsprint and typographical paper throughout this study), included a few other paper types. The demand by these consumers, as calculated in the study, corresponds almost exactly with the amount of paper available:

		x 10³ tons
In 1964, the USSR produced:	Newsprint	632.9
	Paper for multiple uses	34.0
	Typographical paper	249.7
	Offset paper	82.8
	Copper printing paper	72.5
	Lithograph paper	11.2
	TOTAL	1,083.1
In 1964, the USSR exported:	Newsprint	118.8
In 1964, the USSR imported:	Newsprint	46.5
Total available paper supply of types listed above:		1,010.8
Consumption:		1,039.57
Difference:		28.77

(The difference is probably accounted for by the conversion factors used, by Soviet consumption of paper for printing needs in addition to types listed here, or by import of sufficient paper, other than newsprint, to meet this difference.)

Source: Production, 1964. Narodnoye Khozyaystvo SSSR v 1964 godu, p. 198; Export and Import, 1964, Vneshnyaya Torgovlya SSSR za 1964 god, pp. 68-71, 89.

b Pechat' SSSR v 1964 godu, Statisticheskiye Materialy, pp. 109-111; ibid., v 1965 godu, pp. iv, 3. Conversion factor of 51 grams/M² was used to convert to tons.

c Pechat' SSSR v 1964 godu, pp. 85-87. Conversion factor of 99.51 grams/M² was used to convert to tons.

d Ibid., pp. 68, 101-103. Conversion factor of 94.89 grams/M² was used to convert to tons.

e Conversion factor used throughout the study to convert paper into roundwood equivalent is 3.2.

f The West includes Kaliningrad, Pskov, and Smolensk oblasts of the RSFSR.

63

TABLE 21. CHANGES IN MARKET ORIENTATION, 1940-1964
(Measured by Coefficients of Geographic Association)

Association of:	1940	1956	1960	1964
Lumber Production:				
Population	.64	.67	.68	.65
Chemical Pulp Production:				
Population	.33	.31	.32	.35
Paper Production:				
Population	.44	.43	.44	.45

SOURCES: Sources of lumber, chemical pulp, and paper production are given in references to Table 16. Actual population
for 1959 was used for 1956 and 1960. Population for 1939 (used
for 1940) and 1959 was obtained from Itogi Vsesoyuznoy Perepisi
Naseleniya 1959, SSSR, pp. 20-29. Data for 1964 were obtained
from Narodnoye Khozyaystvo SSSR v 1964 godu, pp. 13-21.

production with population in 1940, 1956, 1960, and 1964 on the
basis of their distribution throughout the 16 major Soviet regions
(Table 21). Very little change has occurred in the coefficients
since 1940, implying a steady relationship between the location
of wood-processing and the market. In all wood-processing
industries shown in Table 21, the orientation toward the market
is less than the orientation shown toward the raw material (commercial timber production) in Table 16. The coefficients which
measure the spatial correlation of wood-processing and markets
imply that changes in the distribution of population (market)
have been met by concomitant changes in the distribution of
wood-processing. In both cases there has been at least a
modest shift to the east over the past several decades.

THE MARKET FOR
UNPROCESSED ROUNDWOOD

The distribution of demand for roundwood in unprocessed form
is included to provide a complete statement of the spatial demand for all commercial roundwood in the USSR. This is essential for the subsequent analysis of regional surpluses and
deficits as they relate to the processing industry. The demand
for roundwood in unprocessed form (see note to Table 22) has
been estimated partially on the basis of per capita consumption
and partially on the basis of the distribution of related phenomena (mines and ports). Except in those regions which have a

TABLE 22. THE MARKET FOR ROUNDWOOD
IN UNPROCESSED FORM, 1964

Regions	$M^3(r) \times 10^3$	Per Cent	Per Cent Distribution of USSR Population
USSR	62,278.5	100.0	100.0
RSFSR	34,073.9	54.7	54.9
Northwest	1,439.2	2.3	3.1
Incl. Leningrad Oblast	1,080.4	1.7	2.2
European North	1,876.1	3.0	1.6
Centre	5,803.1	9.6	10.0
Incl. Moscow Oblast	2,033.8	3.6	5.1
Volga-W. Urals	3,339.6	5.3	7.7
Black Earth	2,073.7	3.3	5.2
S. Volga	4,121.7	6.6	6.0
Urals	3,823.5	6.1	5.7
W. Siberia	1,375.9	2.2	3.4
C. Siberia	6,118.7	9.8	4.5
Far East	1,554.3	2.5	1.9
Siberian North	307.0	.5	.5
N. Caucasus	1,665.0	2.6	4.1
Southwest	16,818.6	27.0	21.1
West[a]	3,313.4	5.3	7.7
Caucasus	2,094.0	3.4	4.9
Central Asia	6,564.7	10.5	12.6

SOURCES: The term, Wood Consumed in Unprocessed Form, consists of
pit props, poles, construction wood, ship lumber and marine uses, tanning-
extractive material, material for processing acetic acid, and "others." Although some of this wood may undergo some sort of processing, the distinction
has been made in the study between wood consumed by major processers of
roundwood and wood which, even if processed to a limited degree, is insignificant in the national consumption of roundwood. Poles, construction wood,
and "others" were distributed throughout all regions on a per capita basis.

   Roundwood required for ship lumber and marine uses was assumed to be
consumed in the ports of the USSR (Atlas SSSR, pp. 100-101). For each oblast, kray, or ASSR, the ports (if any) were given a total rating of between 1
(small) and 4 (major) based on general understanding of their function. The
total of all ratings was 71 and, consequently, a port with a rating of 4 was as-
signed 4/71 of the total roundwood required for ship lumber and marine uses.

   Roundwood required for pit props was distributed according to information in Narodnoye Khozyaystvo RSFSR v 1961 godu, p. 127; Narodnoye Khozyaystvo SSSR v 1961 godu, p. 205; Promyshlennost' SSSR, pp. 194-195;
Promyshlennost' RSFSR, p. 76; N. P. Nikitin, ed., Ekonmicheskaya Geografiya SSSR, pp. 95, 98; Yarmola, Voprosy Lesosnabzheniya v SSSR, pp. 178-
179.

   [a]The West includes Kaliningrad, Pskov, and Smolensk oblasts of the
RSFSR.

major share of Soviet coal mining or major port facilities, the
demand for such roundwood could probably have been calculated
reasonably accurately from the distribution of population alone.
However, in the Southwest and Central Siberia, for example,
due to the presence of Donbas and Kuzbas coal mines, the two
percentage distributions vary considerably.

V

The Locational Orientation of Wood-Processing and Associated Flow Patterns

Description of the location of the market for lumber, paper, and roundwood in unprocessed form has been the final step in preparation for the assessment and explanation of the form of the spatial association between component parts of the wood-processing industry. This chapter will measure and evaluate the orientation of aggregate wood-processing activity, saw-milling, and production of pulp and paper, to their raw materials and markets, and will describe and compare the actual and theoretical flows of roundwood and lumber between various regions of the USSR. Determination of the locational orientation is achieved by use of coefficients of simple, multiple, and partial correlation and of geographic association to measure the spatial correspondence between raw materials, markets, and industrial production. Flow patterns are analyzed by comparing actual and theoretically optimal flows of roundwood and lumber between sources of supply and demand.

SPATIAL ASSOCIATION

Coefficients of Correlation
The coefficient of correlation, "r," is one technique used here to measure the degree of the relationship between given var-

iables, i.e., between X and Y where X can be Actual Growing Stock and Y, Total Demand for Roundwood, or X, Total Industrial Production of Wood-Products, and Y, Population, and so forth. Blalock defines "r" as a measure of linear relationship —goodness of fit—of a least squares straight line.[1] The quantity "r" varies between -1 and +1. A strong positive linear correlation will have a value near +1, whereas a strong negative linear correlation will be near -1. A value of "r" near zero indicates the virtual absence of a linear correlation between variables.

Use of the correlation coefficient to measure the relationship between some individual wood-processing industries is not possible since production of many items does not occur in some oblasts, krays, or autonomous republics. This results in a skewed distribution pattern. However, the restrictions imposed by this limitation can be circumvented. By adding two variables together to ensure that some production occurs in every basic region, such as lumber and paper, observations can be obtained for all 85 basic administrative units. Use of paper data alone would have too many zero entries which might seriously reduce the validity of the results.

The correlation coefficients in Table 23 reveal significant differences in the areal association of raw materials, markets, and production. The relationship between all aspects of production and Actual Growing Stock is weak. There is also a very low level of areal association between timber production and population (a rough indication of the final market). Thus, a substantial segment of the processing industry will be unable to take advantage of a location which offers proximity to both raw materials and markets. A choice between the two must be made in the locational orientation (an intermediate location would also be possible). All forms of processing exhibit a strong positive correlation with timber production. The conclusion can therefore be drawn that all wood-processing, despite aggregation in various combinations, shows a strong orientation towards the current location of its chief raw material—roundwood. The areal association between the processing industry and the market (population) is weaker.

Separately, the variables (timber production and market), fail to account for all the statistical variation in the wood-

---

[1]Derivation of simple, multiple, and partial coefficients of correlation is explained well in H. M. Blalock, Jr., Social Statistics, pp. 286-287, 333-336, and 346-350.

processing industry, suggesting thereby that perhaps a combination of variables would account for more of the variation in wood-processing. A coefficient of multiple correlation, R, was calculated with wood-processing as the dependent variable and timber production and market (population) as the independ-

TABLE 23. CORRELATION COEFFICIENTS

	Y_5	Y_6	Y_7	Y_8
X_1 All Wood Processing	.44	.88		.49
X_2 Lumber Production	.43	.82		.57
X_3 Lumber and Pulp Production	.40	.85		.53
X_4 Lumber, Pulp, Paper and Paperboard Production	.38	.85		.53
X_5 Actual Growing Stock		.50	.32	-.04
X_6 Timber Production			.69	.11
X_7 Total Demand for Roundwood by the Processing Industry and in Unprocessed Form				.76
X_8 Population				

NOTE: X_5 and Y_5 denote the same variable, etc.

TABLE 24. COEFFICIENTS OF GEOGRAPHIC ASSOCIATION

	5	6	7	8
1 All Wood Processing	.46	.78		.57
2 Lumber Production	.45	.75		.61
3 Lumber and Pulp Production	.44	.76		.58
4 Lumber, Pulp, Paper and Paperboard Production	.43	.75		.58
5 Actual Growing Stock		.52	.43	.25
6 Timber Production			.69	.38
7 Total Demand for Roundwood by the Processing Industry and in Unprocessed Form				.65
8 Population				

NOTE: Row 5 and Column 5 denote the same variable, etc.

ent variables. The value of R (.96) is high and, when squared, suggests that 92 per cent of the variability in wood-processing is statistically accounted for by the two independent variables. Addition of the variable, Actual Growing Stock, did not produce any measurable change in the value of R or R^2. Evidence of the strong relationship of timber production and the market (population) to wood-processing is further indicated by the high coefficient of partial correlation (.94) between wood-processing and timber production after account is taken of the effect of the market on wood-processing. The coefficient of partial correlation between wood-processing and the market (.84), with the influence of timber production accounted for, is not quite as high as when timber production is the independent variable. The relative importance of each variable here conforms to conclusions drawn above from the simple correlation coefficients. It may be concluded, therefore, that most Soviet wood-processing activity is located at the source of the raw material, at the market, or at both. It appears, therefore, that factors other than raw material and market are not important in the locational orientation of the Soviet wood-processing industry.

Coefficients of Geographic Association

Another measure for comparing the spatial distributions of two phenomena is provided by the coefficient of geographic association. [2]

The coefficients presented in Table 24 permit the same conclusions to be drawn as for the coefficients in Table 23. However, the range between coefficients is greater for correlation than for geographic association, facilitating the identification of significant differences in association. Values of the coefficient of geographic association are .46, .78, .90 and .57 respectively when aggregate wood-processing is measured in turn against actual growing stock, timber production, total demand for roundwood, and population; whereas the same order of correlation coefficients yields .44, .88, .93 and .49.

The coefficients of geographic association in Table 24 in essence represent a similarity or difference in the percentage distribution of two phenomena. When used to measure locational orientation, the coefficients suggest the amount of processing which has a co-location with the raw material, the

[2]Derivation of the coefficient of geographic association is explained in the Notes to Table 16.

market, or both. A coefficient of .38 between timber production and population suggests that 38 per cent of these phenomena is found in the same region. If the processing industry did not locate in these regions, it would have to decide for the remaining 62 per cent to locate near the market or near the raw material. However, 78 per cent of the wood-processing and timber production are found in the same region. This suggests that 40 per cent (78 per cent minus 38 per cent) of wood-processing is at the market alone. Thus, of the 62 per cent (where timber production and population are not found in the same region), 40/62 is accounted for by location of the wood-processing industry at the raw material and 19/62 by location of processing at the market. In this manner, 97 per cent of the industry has been accounted for. The discrepancy of 3 per cent appears to be the result of distortion in the calculations due to the production of roundwood which is destined for consumption in inprocessed form.

Roundwood: Regional
Surplus and Deficit

Table 25 summarizes data for 85 administrative units, of which 56 are wood-deficient and 29 are wood-surplus. Adjustment of the volume of timber cut to compensate for net exports (exports out of the USSR plus the small volume of roundwood imported) yields a figure for regional supply. Regional demand minus regional supply yields a figure for regional supply. Regional demand minus regional supply yields a figure of surplus or deficit for each region. Aggregation of deficits for each of the 85 basic regions shows that a total of 80,698,970 M^3 must be shipped from one administrative unit to another to satisfy internal demand within the USSR. This figure is 30 per cent of the total amount of roundwood consumed within the USSR. In other words, nearly one-third of all wood consumed within the country must cross an oblast, kray, or autonomous republic boundary before it can be used. The same aggregate measure can be derived from Table 24. Timber production and total demand for roundwood by the processing industry and in unprocessed form have a coefficient of .69 which implies that 69 per cent of these phenomena is found in the same region and 31 per cent is found separately. The 1 per cent difference between 30 per cent and 31 per cent is caused by the use of regional timber

70

production instead of regional timber supply (production net of exports) in Table 24.

As the data are presented in Table 25, the types of consumer in each region are not distinguished. It is quite possible that only certain industries in any given region require round-wood from outside the region, while all other industries or consumers obtain their timber supply locally. Thus, in any region, some wood-processing plants may be oriented to their raw material, while others are oriented to their market. In other cases, a single consumer may obtain various grades of timber from local suppliers while purchasing different grades in other areas. With the great number of consumers involved and the number of different log grades and sizes which come onto the market, some roundwood may be shipped into areas identified as having a surplus of raw material. In addition, it must be noted that of the 268 million M^3 of roundwood consumed, about 23 per cent (or 62 million M^3) did not pass through processing plants, i.e., was consumed in unprocessed form. It is not possible to determine what proportion of the minimum inter-oblast shipment of 80 million M^3 consisted of timber in this category. However, despite the limitations which are placed on this study by a lack of specific Soviet data, the basic problem of supplying over 80 million M^3 of roundwood to markets in 56 regions still remains.

Lumber: Regional
Surplus and Deficit

The data presented in Table 26 show the amount of lumber which is surplus or deficit in any region. Lumber consumption is estimated on a per capita basis. These estimates indicate 44 deficit regions and 40 surplus regions in the USSR (if Magadan and Kamchatka are combined). When the volume of lumber sawn is adjusted to compensate for national Soviet exports and the small volume of deciduous lumber imported, a total of 37,930,000 M^3 must be shipped from one administrative unit to another to satisfy internal demand within the USSR. This figure (almost 37 per cent) signifies that nearly two-fifths of all lumber consumed in the USSR has been transported between oblasts, krays, or autonomous republics to consumers. If these estimates are valid, it is also evident that approximately three-fifths of Soviet lumber is cut near the consumer. This suggests two possible forms of locational orientation for such sawmills:

71

TABLE 25.   REGIONAL SURPLUSES AND DEFICITS OF COMMERCIAL TIMBER, 1964 (M^3[r] x 10^3)

Regions	(1) Timber Cut[a]	(2) Net Exports[b]	(3) Regional Timber Supply (1) - (2)	(4) Regional Demand[c] (Total Consumption)	(5) Surplus[d] (3 > 4)	(6) Deficit[e] (3 < 4)
USSR	276,874	8,715	268,159	268,159		
RSFSR	255,888		247,173	204,249	42,924	
Northwest	24,911	1,277	23,634	17,893	5,741	
European North	47,121	3,495	43,626	22,738	20,888	5,670
Centre	16,743		16,743	22,413		5,670
Volga-W. Urals	32,296	466	31,830	25,451	6,379	
Black Earth	3,057		3,057	6,071		3,014
S. Volga	1,137		1,137	11,027		9,890
Urals	48,319	932	47,387	29,614	17,774	
W. Siberia	11,467		11,467	9,714	1,753	
C. Siberia	48,644	88	48,556	37,472	11,084	
Far East	15,236	2,428	12,808	11,687	1,121	
Siberian North	1,881	30	1,851	1,554	297	
N. Caucasus	2,834		2,834	5,173		2,339
Southwest	9,027		9,027	32,671		23,644
West	12,260		12,260	17,898		5,638
Caucasus	687		687	4,135		3,448
Central Asia	1,254		1,254	12,646		11,392
SUM of Regional Units					65,037	65,037
SUM of Regional Sub Units (Oblasts, Krays, and ASSR's)					80,699	80,699

NOTE: Figures have been rounded from two decimal places. Values for regional sub units have been omitted from Tables 25 and 26 but are contained in B. M. Barr, "The Role of Transfer Costs in the Location and Flow Patterns of The Soviet Wood-Processing Industry" (unpublished Ph.D. dissertation, Department of Geography, University of Toronto, 1968), pp. 144-148, 152-156.

a Narodnoye Khozyaystvo RSFSR v 1964 godu, pp. 90-93; Narodnoye Khozyaystvo SSSR v 1964 godu, pp. 194-195.

b Vneshnaya Torgovlya SSSR za 1964 god, p. 32. Amount of roundwood exported from any oblast, kray, or ASSR was derived chiefly from the following: Yarmola, Voprosy Lesnogo Snabzheniya v SSSR, p. 18; Nechuyatova, Geograficheskoye Razmeshcheniye Derevoobrabatyvayushchey Promyshlennosti SSSR, pp. 113, 141, 148; Soviet Union Today, October, 1966, p. 33; Gorovoy and Privalovskaya, Geografiya Lesnoy Promyshlennosti SSSR, pp. 131-132; Lesnaya Promyshlennost', No. 94, 1964, p. 1, and No. 131, 1964, p. 4.

c Includes the roundwood equivalent of all wood products produced in each region plus the roundwood consumed in unprocessed form in each region.

d The result of subtracting total consumption from timber cut, in each region where supply exceeds demand.

e The result of subtracting total consumption from timber cut, in each region where demand exceeds supply.

TABLE 26.   REGIONAL SURPLUSES AND DEFICITS OF LUMBER, 1964 (M³ × 10³)

Regions	(1) Lumber Sawn[a]	(2) Net Exports[b]	(3) Regional Lumber Supply (1) − (2)	(4) Regional Demand (Total Consumption)[c]	(5) Surplus (3) − (4)	(6) Deficit (3) − (4)
USSR	110,899	7,432	103,467	103,467		
RSFSR	90,189	7,676	82,513	56,775	25,738	
Northwest	7,313	795	6,518	3,209	3,309	
European North	10,565	5,892	4,674	1,651	3,022	
Centre	9,694		9,694	10,356		662
Volga–W. Urals	12,698	63	12,635	7,946	4,689	
Black Earth	2,416		2,416	5,426		3,010
S. Volga	4,484		4,484	6,214		1,730
Urals	12,739	126	12,613	5,872	6,741	
W. Siberia	4,722		4,722	3,527	1,195	
C. Siberia	16,799	800	15,999	4,614	11,385	
Far East	4,744		4,744	1,918	2,826	
Siberian North	810		810	531	279	
N. Caucasus	2,233		2,233	4,308		2,075
Southwest	9,746	-244	9,980	21,850		11,860
West	6,772		6,772	7,973		1,201
Caucasus	1,215		1,215	5,027		3,812
Central Asia	3,949		3,949	13,045		9,096
SUM of Regional Units					33,446	33,446
SUM of Regional Sub Units (Oblasts, Krays and ASSR's)					37,930	37,930

[a]Narodnoye Khozyaystvo RSFSR v 1964 godu, pp. 95-96; Narodnoye Khozyaystvo SSSR v 1964 godu, p. 197.

[b]Vneshnyaya Torgovlya SSSR za 1964 god, pp. 68-71. Amount of lumber exported from (or imported by) any oblast, kray, or ASSR was derived chiefly from the following: Yarmola, Voprosy Lesosnabzheniya v SSSR, p. 18; Nechuyatova, Geograficheskoye Razmeshcheniye Derevoobrabatyvayushchey Promyshlennosti SSSR, pp. 112, 121, 141, 147-148, 232-233; Soviet Union Today, October, 1966, p. 33. Help on this problem was kindly provided by Mr. J. Holowacz.

[c]Derived on the basis of per capita consumption, 1964, which was estimated in the following manner:

		x 10³
1. USSR production:		110,899.00
2. USSR export:		7,675.60
3. USSR import:		243.70
4. Net amount available:		103,467.10
5. Population:		229,198.00
6. M³ / person, i.e.,		
	No. 4/No. 5 = .45143	

Therefore, for each region, multiply the population by .45143 M³ to obtain an estimate of total consumption of lumber.

location near the consumer using local roundwood, or location near the consumer using roundwood transported from other regions. As Soviet plans continually call for location of sawmilling nearer to the source of timber, it is assumed here that a significant proportion of the Soviet sawmilling industry which is located near the market consumes roundwood which has been transported from other regions.

INTERREGIONAL FLOWS

Actual Flows of Roundwood and Lumber

Actual interregional movements in 1964 of roundwood and lumber between 34 regions were estimated from data obtained for 1963.[3] These estimates are given in Appendices B and E.

The importance of Appendices B and E is two-fold. Many regions ship to the same consumer and many consumers receive shipments from a wide range of suppliers. In the optimum solutions obtained by linear programming techniques, the number of suppliers per region is drastically reduced. Secondly, and of greater importance, is the question which arises from a close inspection of these tables, "Is the actual pattern of roundwood and lumber movement more efficient than the theoretical movement?" Recent studies by Soviet scholars who have considered this question suggest that the plans for the actual flow of coal in the USSR and cement in the Ukraine differ significantly from the theoretical flows derived through linear programming when all products are highly aggregated. However, when special differences in grades are considered, calculated savings based on the theoretical flows are considerably reduced.[4] Obviously, in the forest industry, not all wood and lumber are of the same grade or same species. A high degree of substitution between species does exist, however, and more penetrating comparisons of actual and theoretical flows would be possible if provision were made for special flows of, for example, birch to plywood mills, etc. Flows which now may appear as uneconomic or irrational might be justified on the basis of fundamental differences in the characteristics of species and products. However, the composition of actual flows

[3] I. S. Yarmola, Voprosy Lesosnabzheniya v SSSR, pp. 170-177.

[4] J. P. Hardt, et al., eds., Mathematics and Computers in Soviet Economic Planning, pp. 160-176.

76

cannot be determined from available data; nor can the regional demand by species be estimated. In addition, the sources of supply and demand are fixed in the present calculations, thereby reducing the disparity between actual and theoretical flows. It is quite probable that significant deviations would occur between the origin and destination of actual and theoretical flows if the model optimized the location of supply and demand.

The Transportation Problem

It is important in transporting materials between spatially separated points to organize shipments so as to minimize the total cost of transportation.[5] In this study, actual interregional flows of roundwood and lumber are presented. However, based on surpluses and deficits, the task of assigning materials to consumers can be formulated as a type of transportation problem, which in turn can be solved as a linear programming problem.

Suppose that the state manufactures a certain type of plywood in n (three) mills at different locations in the country, and that this plywood is distributed to m (five) furniture factories in other parts of the country. Total production per day, 15 tons, is to be distributed among the plywood mills (producing 6, 6, and 3 tons) and the five furniture factories (requiring 4, 2, 2, 4, and 3 tons). What is an optimal pattern of shipments (i.e., the pattern in which the total cost of transportation is minimal)? The problem is to minimize the total transport cost, T, for shipments of plywood, X, from plywood mill i to furniture factory j. Summation for each mill-factory pair (ij) of the transport cost per ton of plywood (C_{ij}) multiplied by the size of the shipment (X_{ij}), will yield the minimum total cost of transportation, T.

Some form of aggregation of the physical units to be shipped (X_{ij}) multiplied by the respective transport cost (C_{ij}) will yield a minimum value for the objective function, "T." Thus,

$$T = \text{minimum} = \sum_i \sum_j C_{ij}X_{ij}$$

where T is the total cost of transportation, subject to the conditions that:

supply and demand are equal,

[5]For a full discussion of the formulation and solution of the Transportation Problem, the reader is referred to the sources and presentation in B. M. Barr, "The Role of Transfer Costs in the Location and Flow Patterns of the Soviet Wood-Processing Industry" (unpublished Ph.D. dissertation, University of Toronto, 1968), pp. 160-179.

$$\sum_{i=1}^{n} X_{ij} = \sum_{j=1}^{m} X_{ij}$$

and that production and demand are not negative:

$$X_{ij} \geq 0$$

The unknown values, the X_{ij}, are tons per day. They have corresponding cost coefficients, C_{ij}, which may be thought of as the Ruble cost per ton shipped from the $\underline{i}$ th origin to the $\underline{j}$ th destination.

Every linear programme formulated as a minimum has a dual problem formulated in terms of a maximum, and vice versa. Using the same data, in one problem the results are to be minimized whereas in the other problem the results are to be maximized. Solution of the dual has important economic implications because it represents imputed values, based on marginal costs, and provides a means for placing an economic value on inputs and outputs. The function of the dual in the transportation problem is to maximize the price of products at the factory and to maximize the income received for these products at the market. In other words, the dual to the transportation problem provides a technique for estimating the relative differences in factory price and marketed price among different producers and consumers. Factory and delivered prices correspond to the optimum pattern of shipments based on minimum aggregate transportation costs; these prices can be compared with actual relative prices at various factories and markets, just as optimal shipments between factories and markets can be compared with real shipments.

In this study, the largest formulations have 28 sources and 56 sinks (destinations) for roundwood shipments and 40 sources and 44 sinks for lumber shipments.[6] The method of solution of the transportation problem in the study follows the approach recommended by Balinski and Gomory.[7] An IBM computer programme, based on their method, was used to solve the transportation problem.

[6] Although the number of basic regions used in the study is 85, only 84 regions enter the linear programming formulation. It has been assumed that Kamchatka's surplus of roundwood is entirely exported and that Magadan and Kamchatka together constitute one regional unit in shipping their lumber surplus to markets within the USSR.

[7] M. L. Balinski and R. E. Gomory, "A Primal Method for the Assignment and Transportation Problems," Management Science, X (April, 1964), 578-593.

Preparation for
Linear Programming
The basis for preparing a matrix of transportation costs between regions of supply and demand is the distance matrix of short-line rail distances, in kilometres, between all regions of the USSR. [8] In some cases administrative centres have been used, while in others centres more representative of the area from which wood shipments might be expected to occur have been chosen. A matrix of transportation costs per M^3 between regions was calculated for each linear programming problem from pertinent railway transport tariffs. [9] Each matrix includes the supply or demand for each region.

Actual and Theoretical Flows
Roundwood. The theoretical shipments of roundwood shown in Appendix A have been prepared from the calculations of regional surpluses and deficits summarized in Table 25. The function of Appendix A is to provide a statement of the optimum interregional movement of roundwood when oblasts, krays, and autonomous republics are used as basic statistical units. Unfortunately, it is still impossible to obtain actual roundwood flows for such a large regional matrix.

Actual flows of commercial timber, arranged in a 34 x 34 regional matrix, have been obtained for 1963. [10] The 34 regional units employed permit detailed evaluation of the major patterns of roundwood flows in the USSR. As the production data employed in the study are for 1964, the 1963 flow data have been interpolated for 1964 by increasing the total 1963 production of 241,261,100 M^3 shown in Yarmola to the 1964 total of 276,874,000 M^3 and making corresponding adjustments for all regional totals. Thus, as production in 1964 is 114.76 per cent greater than in 1963, each total regional production figure was multiplied by 1.1476.

The estimated total regional production of commercial timber for each of the 34 regions was distributed throughout all regions using the same percentage figures as those associated with such shipments in 1963 (Appendix B).

---

[8] The distance matrix was compiled from distances between cities shown on the map, Skhema Zheleznykh Dorog SSSR, and checked against distances shown on maps in the atlas, Zheleznye Dorogi SSSR, Napravleniya i Stantsii.

[9] Comprehensive schedules of railway tariffs actually used in the USSR are given in A. S. Arkhangel'skiy, comp., Spravochnik po Tarifam Zheleznodorozhnogo Transporta.

[10] Yarmola, Voprosy Lesosnabzheniya, pp. 170-177.

The figures of total regional production given by Yarmola are somewhat lower than actual production of commercial timber in each region in 1963. Yarmola obviously excludes timber cut by certain agencies (perhaps by collective farms whose cut, in principle, is for local consumption), or does not include roundwood consumed at or near the site of production. This slight discrepancy does not reduce the usefulness of Yarmola's data for evaluating actual and theoretical patterns of roundwood movement in the USSR.

The supply or demand for each region in Appendix C corresponds to the actual surplus or deficit for each region in Appendix A. In the latter, for example, the Northwest region is shown to produce $45,086 \times 10^3$ M^3 of roundwood annually, while the total amount of roundwood shipped to consumers in the Northwest, from within the region itself or from other regions, is $29,253 \times 10^3$ M^3. The net demand for roundwood is, therefore, $29,253 \times 10^3$ M^3 and $15,833 \times 10^3$ M^3 appear as the regional surplus in Appendix C. The Moscow region produces $5,438 \times 10^3$ M^3 of roundwood annually but receives a total of $9,579 \times 10^3$ M^3 (Appendix B), thus registering a net deficit of $4,141 \times 10^3$ M^3 in Appendix C. The diagonal in Appendix B is the amount of roundwood supplied by each region to itself. The underlined figures in Appendix B indicate similarity in direction between theoretical and actual flow movements although the actual amounts involved are not the same. Flows represented by numbers which are not underlined in Appendix B do not exist in the optimal movement pattern in Appendix C.

At first glance, comparison of the flows in Appendix B with those in Appendix C indicates that the optimal pattern is quite different from the actual one. However, Appendix B contains numerous small shipments of roundwood which, taken separately or together, account for a very small portion of the total roundwood movement. Figure 7 (based on Appendix B containing shipments greater than 250,000 M^3 per annum) appears remarkably similar to Figure 8 (based on Appendix C) in general orientation of flows, length of flows, and origin-destination links. This suggests that the allocation of roundwood in the linear programming example (Appendix C) follows the same economic dictates as actual allocation of the significant shipments by Soviet planners. When flows smaller than 250,000 M^3 are added to Figure 7, the pattern becomes confused by cross and back hauls. The great number of small shipments obscure the

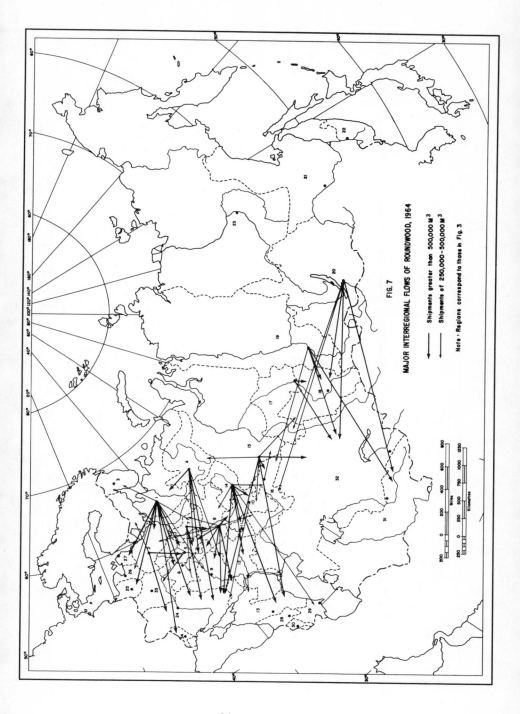

MAJOR INTERREGIONAL FLOWS OF ROUNDWOOD, 1964

Shipments greater than 500,000 M³

Shipments of 250,000 - 500,000 M³

Note : Regions correspond to those in Fig. 3

FIG. 7

81

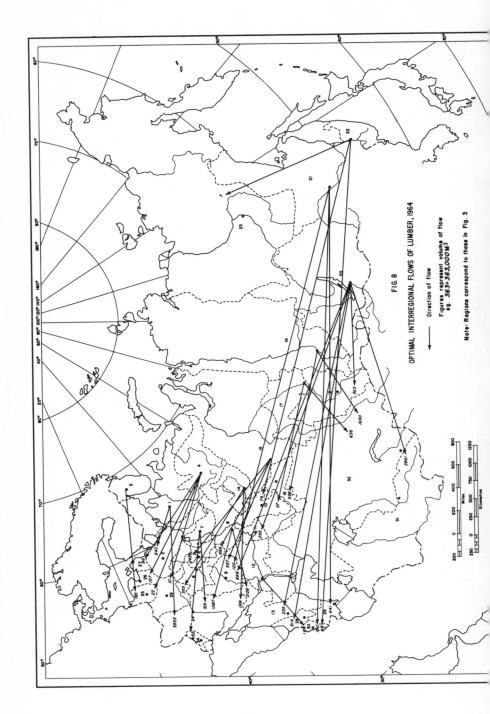

FIG. 8

OPTIMAL INTERREGIONAL FLOWS OF LUMBER, 1964

→ Direction of flow

Figures represent volume of flow
eg. *363-363,000M³*

Note: Regions correspond to those in Fig. 3

82

general processes at work and, due to their heterogeneity, cause the <u>total</u> pattern of actual hauls to be oriented quite differently from the optimal flows presented in Figure 8.

How are the differences between actual and theoretical flows to be explained? Some of the observed differences probably are accounted for by the movement of different species. In this study, it has been assumed that all roundwood is of the same sort of species, i.e., that various species could be substituted one for another. Even if this were true, some movement of birch and aspen for production of plywood would tend to distort a perfect theoretical pattern. But apart from errors in the assumptions of the model, the differences between actual and theoretical flows appear to be caused by imperfections in the Soviet central planning techniques. One of those techniques should be to derive a pattern of minimal transportation costs in the movement of roundwood to consumers. Even if the location of productive forces is not optimal, it is evident that the pattern of flows between logging enterprises and wood-processing plants could be successfully rearranged. Perhaps some of the differences could be explained if more data had been obtained on river movements of roundwood and on the cost structure of shipment by rafts and barges. However, the following data indicate that the observed differences between actual and theoretical movements (for pairs of tables) would probably be much the same even if all flow patterns had their total aggregate cost proportionately reduced by introducing river shipments into the pattern (Table 27).

The savings achieved by the theoretical pattern in Appendix C in comparison with the actual flow pattern in Appendix B, amount to nearly 55 million rubles or a reduction of 20 per cent. It is also evident that the amounts shipped in the theoretical patterns often are less than in reality because the theoretical shipments, by definition, preclude the heterogeneity of demand which is revealed in the form of cross hauls in the pattern of actual flows.

The solution of the dual of the transportation problem yields f.o.b. prices which could be obtained per unit of roundwood at the point of supply and c.i.f. prices which could be obtained at the market. The f.o.b. price per unit of roundwood at any point of supply, plus the unit costs of transportation from origin to destination, equals the c.i.f. price at the market. Solution to the dual of the transportation problem provides

83

TABLE 27. TOTAL SHIPMENT COSTS OF
VARIOUS FLOW PATTERNS OF ROUNDWOOD

Appendix	Title	Matrix Size	Volume Shipped M³ x 10⁶	Total Shipping Cost (Current Rubles) x 10⁶	Cost Rank
A	"Optimum Shipments of Round-wood between Oblasts, Krays, and Autonomous Republics" (By linear programming)	28 origins 56 destinations	80.7	324.3	3
B	"Actual Interregional Movement of Roundwood" (After Yarmola)	34 origins 34 destinations	72.7	279.2	2
C	"Optimum Interregional Shipment of Roundwood" (By linear programming)	12 origins 22 destinations	57.7	224.7	1

a system of equilibrium prices for the entire Soviet Union. In
Appendices A and C, the prices provided are equilibrium prices
and shipments other than those indicated would result in higher
c.i.f. prices. For example, in Appendix A, Leningrad oblast
is included in the optimum shipment plan of the Karelia ASSR
$(1,243,000$ M³). The transportation cost of 1 M³ of roundwood between Karelia and Leningrad is 1.6 Rubles. Thus, the
f.o.b. price in Karelia, R22.0, plus the transportation cost to
Leningrad, R1.6, equals the c.i.f. price in Leningrad of R23.6.
The same relationship prevails for all origin-destination links
shown in Appendices A and C. If, in Appendix A, roundwood
were shipped to Moscow from Karelia, the c.i.f. price in Moscow would exceed the equilibrium price. Thus, the f.o.b. price
in Karelia, R22.0, plus the transportation cost to Moscow, R2.2,
equals R24.2 which exceeds the equilibrium c.i.f. price in Moscow of R23.4.

The system of equilibrium prices obtained from the dual of
the transportation problem provides a situation in which further
shipments from any destination to any origin not included in the
equilibrium situation cannot be made at a profit. In the real
world, it is reasonable to expect such an equilibrium situation
to exist, although the absolute level of prices in all regions may
vary from period to period depending on the amount of roundwood
offered for sale. The theoretical equilibrium prices in Appen-

84

dices A and C could be compared with the actual prices existing in all regions of the USSR to evaluate the degree to which Soviet pricing policies have brought about a condition of spatial equilibrium. Unfortunately, reliable Soviet regional price figures could not be obtained in Moscow and this part of the analysis must be left for further research and investigation until such a time as sufficient data become available.

These imputed f.o.b. and c.i.f. prices in themselves, however, do not serve as an adequate basis on which to assess the merits of recent regional shifts in timber production. They have been derived from an abstracted system of surpluses and deficits, and they do not include other cost considerations such as regional labour costs, raw material costs, stumpage fees, and operating expenses. The highest f.o.b. prices in Appendix A are found in Smolensk, Kalinin, Gorki, and Pskov oblasts, all of which have registered a levelling off or reduction in timber production in recent years. In addition, these four oblasts have a surplus of roundwood which is shipped to other regions! Although a tapering off of f.o.b. prices toward the Far East is noticeable from Appendix A, only limited meaning can be derived. The prices indicate nothing about the prices of timber consumed locally. If more timber were cut in the Far East, for example, resulting in a greater surplus, and less in Central Siberia, perhaps the imputed prices in the Far East would be different. Finally, the imputed prices cannot serve as completely reliable indicators of the need for a regional shift in timber production as nothing is known about the elasticity of demand for competing products. These imputed prices are included here for completeness in the hope that useful actual regional price data might soon become available.

Lumber. Calculation of actual and theoretical flows of lumber shipments between regions has been organized in a similar manner to that of roundwood flows. Optimum lumber shipments between all oblasts, krays, and autonomous republics are shown in Appendix D. Although data for actual flows at such a disaggregated level have not been obtained, identification of optimum flows for all basic statistical units provides a basis of comparison with more aggregated lumber flows. The total cost of disaggregated flows, against that of more aggregated costs, provides a measure of the loss of precision through aggregation. An equilibrium price solution is also given in Appendix D.

Appendix E was derived by the same method as Appendix B. The method used to obtain the regional surpluses and deficits

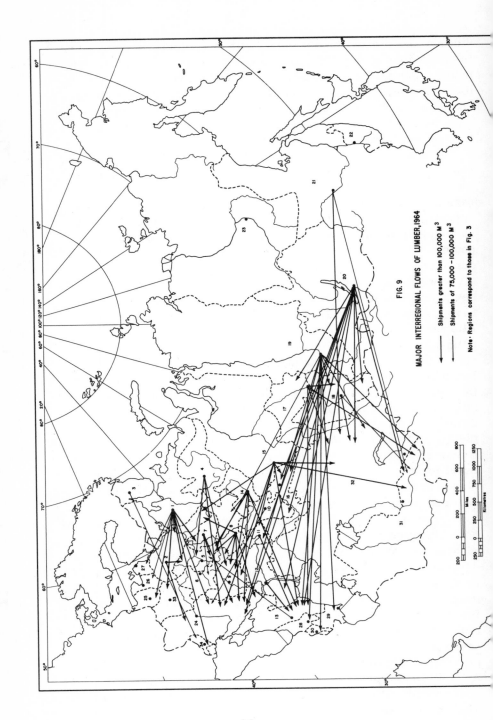

MAJOR INTERREGIONAL FLOWS OF LUMBER,1964

→ Shipments greater than 100,000 M³

→ Shipments of 75,000 – 100,000 M³

Note: Regions correspond to those in Fig. 3

FIG. 9

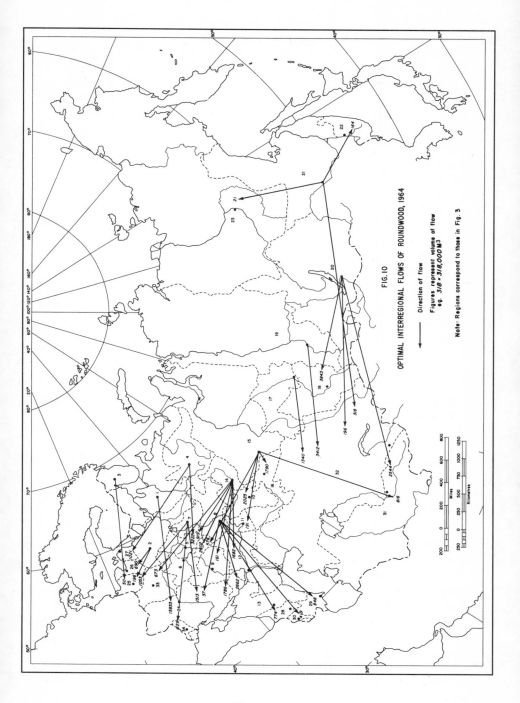

FIG. 10

OPTIMAL INTERREGIONAL FLOWS OF ROUNDWOOD, 1964

→ Direction of flow

Figures represent volume of flow
eg. 3/8 = 318,000 M³

Note: Regions correspond to those in Fig. 3

in Appendix F is completely analagous to that used in Appendix C. The same wide discrepancy between actual and theoretical flows which was observed for roundwood shipments is evident in Appendices E and F. Those shipments in Appendix E which correspond to the direction of optimal shipments in Appendix F have been underlined. The diagonal represents the shipments of a region to itself. In Appendix E, actual shipments out of a region do not preclude the shipment of lumber into the region; many regions with a net deficit record some outward shipments. This element of cross and back hauls is, by definition, not permissible in the theoretical pattern. Comparison of the flows in Figure 9 (based on Appendix E) with those in Figure 10 (based on Appendix F) reveals, however, that considerable similarity in significant flows does exist between the actual and optimal patterns. Figure 9, containing shipments greater than 75,000 M^3 per annum, displays close resemblance to Figure 10 in length of hauls, orientation of flows, and origin-destination links, suggesting the same sort of orientation between significant actual and theoretical lumber shipments as was previously noted for roundwood (Figures 7 and 8). When hauls smaller than 75,000 M^3 are added to Figure 10, the pattern changes due to cross and back hauls. It should be noted that back hauls could represent the movement of lumber of one type into a region which exports lumber of a different type. But this fact does not appear to explain fully the very wide discrepancy in orientation between total actual and theoretical flows.

The total cost of transportation in Appendices D, E, and F, is presented in Table 28. The saving in total transport costs in the theoretical shipments is significant. Arranging flows in Appendix E according to the optimal solution in Appendix F saves approximately 16 million rubles, a reduction of 12 per cent over the actual flow pattern. The attainment of such a reduction in total shipment costs probably would never occur in reality because the technique for estimating optimal flows assumes that no cross-hauls occur in response to differences between species. While this is not out of keeping with methods used in most theoretical studies, the calculated savings do appear to be too large. However, if the output and input mix for every region were known, a more realistic set of flows could be programmed to achieve the maximum total saving.

A system of equilibrium prices for lumber, derived from the dual of the transportation problem in the same manner as

TABLE 28. TOTAL SHIPMENT COSTS OF
VARIOUS FLOW PATTERNS OF LUMBER

Appendix	Title	Matrix Size	Volume Shipped M^3 x 10^6	Total Shipping Cost (Current Rubles) x 10^6	Cost Rank
D	"Optimum Shipment of Lumber between Oblasts, Krays, and Autonomous Republics" (By linear programming)	40 origins 44 destinations	37.9	206.5	3
E	"Actual Interregional Movement of Lumber" (After Yarmola)	34 origins 34 destinations	26.7	133.8	2
F	"Optimum Interregional Shipment of Lumber" (By linear programming)	13 origins 21 destinations	24.1	117.9	1

those for roundwood, is presented in Appendices D and F. The
same relationship between f.o.b. prices, transport costs, and
c.i.f. prices exists in these tables as in the tables of similar
prices for roundwood. Although actual regional prices have not
been obtained for lumber, the theoretical equilibrium prices
are included here because they represent an important potential
statement of the type of regional price equilibrium which should
exist in reality. Judging by the increasing amount of statistical
information emanating from the Soviet Union, there is a distinct
probability that in the near future comparisons between the imputed prices derived here and actual prices might be possible.

VI

Transportation Costs and the Location of Wood-Processing

The empirical and theoretical flows of roundwood and lumber suggest that a significant portion of Soviet forest products moves a considerable distance before being consumed in a final form. Much of the wood moving within any economic region is shipped by river (barge and raft), while interregional shipments largely go by rail (Table 29). The concern of this study has been with interregional movements of roundwood and lumber, and consequently with the effect of railway tariff policies on the cost of moving these products. It is necessary, therefore, to examine the concepts underlying Soviet rail freight rates (particularly with reference to the rates on wood products), and to analyze the relationship of Soviet rail tariffs to the location of wood-processing industries.

MEASUREMENT AND DATA

Much has been written on Soviet rates but the actual rates themselves are difficult to obtain. Tariff manuals for particular railroads are classified information in the USSR and the public does not have access to these manuals. In North America, rates vary from railroad to railroad and identical mileage between various sets of places does not mean that the economic distance, as expressed by rail rates, is the same. In the So-

TABLE 29. TOTAL MOVEMENT OF FOREST PRODUCTS
INCLUDING FUELWOOD BETWEEN REPUBLICS AND OFFICIAL
MAJOR ECONOMIC REGIONS, 1965 (Tons x 10^6)

Region		Railroad	Sea	River	Total
USSR Export (To Other Districts)		(86.4%)	(.6%)	(13.0%)	
		98.57	.67	14.73	113.97
Import (From Other Districts)		96.89	1.12	14.65	112.66
		(86.0%)	(1.0%)	(13.0%)	
Northwest	Export	30.00	.52	1.33	31.85
	Import	2.22		.02	2.24
Centre	Export	4.44		2.60	7.04
	Import	10.85		.57	11.42
Volga-Vyatka	Export	11.29		2.23	13.52
	Import	1.54		1.51	3.05
Central Black Earth	Export			.01	.01
	Import	5.30			5.30
Volga-Littoral	Export	4.62	.11	.99	5.72
	Import	6.58		8.92	15.50
North Caucasus	Export	1.61			1.61
	Import	7.39	.24	2.39	10.02
Urals	Export	17.01		7.06	24.07
	Import	1.86		.02	1.88
Western Siberia	Export	5.61		.21	5.82
	Import	3.94		.07	4.01
Eastern Siberia	Export	21.86	.01	.15	22.02
	Import	.29	.02	.02	.33
Far East	Export	1.13		.02	1.15
	Import	.27	.12	.08	.47
Ukraine	Export			.02	.02
	Import	29.68	.01	.09	29.78
Moldavia	Export				0.00
	Import	1.84			1.84
Baltic States	Export	.50			.50
	Import	4.35	.56	.40	5.31
Byelorussia	Export	.50		.10	.60
	Import	2.43		.35	2.78
Caucasus	Export		.01		.01
	Import	3.72	.11		3.83
Central Asia	Export		.02	.01	.03
	Import	14.63	.06	.21	14.90

SOURCE: Transport i Svyaz' SSSR, Statisticheskiy Sbornik, pp. 68–69, 86–89.
NOTES: The difference between departures and arrivals (1.31 million tons) is not accounted
for in the source. The difference could be explained as the amount of wood in transit at
year end.

Greater arrivals by sea than departures could perhaps be explained as receipt of wood
shipped in the previous year (1964).

Total exports (113.97 x 10^6 tons) have an approximate volume of 163 x 10^6 M^3.

Total imports (112.66 x 10^6 tons) have an approximate volume of 161 x 10^6 M^3.

Figures are presented according to the system of Official Major Economic Regions used
in the source handbook.

viet Union, however, except for a few special agreements between some shippers and the Ministry of Railways, the distance between two points is a realistic guide for determining the cost of transportation of any item between these two points. Consequently, a tariff manual summarizing the current mileage rates for major items has been used as the basis for all transport-cost calculations in this study.[1] Revisions in Soviet freight rates since 1917 have been frequent and the rates currently applicable were introduced in 1955. Changes to these rates, although recommended in 1961, have not yet been carried out.

RAILWAY TARIFFS

National railway tariffs usually reflect political forces and economic policies of each national unit. Tariffs are structured to bring about the ends desired by those groups who have the most political (and consequently, economic) influence over the railways. In North America, the railways have been subjected to increasing government control since World War I and freight rate policies have ceased to be the prerogative solely of the railways concerned. In the USSR, over the same period, the railways have been completely administered by the state; rate policies have been set by political and planning authorities. In both societies, however, implementation of the rates is carried out by the railways.

A prime component of Soviet rates is the cost of providing the service, whereas in Canada, for example, rates are chiefly based on the ability of commodities to bear the cost of transportation. Because many other factors interact in both countries to influence rates, it is instructive to discuss the characteristics of Soviet freight rates by suggesting pertinent comparisons with Canadian rating principles. Such an assessment will add perspective to some of the peculiarities which exist in Soviet freight rates.

[1] Arkhangel'skiy, comp., Spravochnik po Tarifam Zheleznodorozhnogo Transporta (reprinted without significant changes, 1964). The basic tariff manual containing transportation costs of all items between all places in the USSR, Preyskurant No. 10-01, Tarifov na gruzovye zheleznodorozhnye perevozki, was refused this author in the Lenin library.

Individual Plants and
Transportation Costs

Freight rates do not have the same significance to Soviet producers as to Canadian producers. In the USSR, rates act as a basis by which the Ministry of Railways can collect monetary payment for services rendered, and rates play some role in planning the location of wood-processing plants. In Canada, the rate obtained for marketing or assembling a particular commodity is very significant to the degree of profitability of production at any location. Transport charges in the USSR lose their significance to a buyer. Consumers of industrial goods who pay prices and transport costs specified in their supply plan are not influenced in the regional origin of purchases by transport charges. Such charges are significant only to planning circles. Transportation costs are items over which the managers of individual plants appear to have little or no control. Pressure to ensure that freight rates have any degree of economic meaning comes only from planners.

In the wood-processing industry where weight-loss during processing is of key significance, the freight rates associated with production are very important in choosing a site for processing. In the USSR, this aspect of transport costs is of practically no significance to the shipper or receiver as such costs are already built into the state plan and into the delivery schedules of every enterprise. Both the initial locational decision affecting the distribution of the processing plants, and the flow patterns associated with those plants, fall under the jurisdiction of the central planning agencies. The rates may be structured in part to reflect predetermined conceptions of suitable patterns of location. Once rate levels have been established, it appears that one important role of those planning the location of wood-processing is to minimize total costs to the entire system, both in selecting locations for processing plants and in scheduling the interregional flows of roundwood and processed products insofar as such action does not hinder realization of other objectives. The rates do not reflect a multitude of independent forces working constantly, as in Canada, to rearrange the spatial organization of all industry. Canadian railways are revenue-earning enterprises which attempt to maximize profits. That is, they are an independent operation transporting goods as a service. One of their prime functions, however, is not to be an instrument of the state, or business at large, in planning the location of productive forces. Applied in the planning process, however, Soviet rates do have an impact on the spatial distribution of any industry.

Soviet freight rates are the best uniform criteria available to Soviet planners for estimating the costs of transporting wood and wood products between suppliers and consumers. However, the impact of the rates on the location of the wood-processing industry appears to be tempered by a desire to achieve overall objectives of the state plan. These objectives may entail overexpenditure on some items (such as transport costs) in order to achieve the major goal. Thus, other cost considerations and political objectives may conflict with the objective of minimizing transport costs (for example, the desire to provide additional manufacturing employment in a wood-deficit region such as Central Asia or the Ukraine; or the high cost of construction and unfavourable living conditions in parts of wood-surplus regions such as Central Siberia, the Siberian North, or the Far East).

The significance of Soviet freight rates as a planning tool means that they are an appropriate base for assessing the cost of freight movements, despite the fact that rates are not set by the free play of market forces. Transportation costs can be combined with weight-loss factors to determine the most economic orientation of the wood-processing industry (raw material versus market) in terms of transfer costs. Insights can be obtained into the relative roles which transport costs and other factors have played in locational decisions by examining the actual locational orientation.

Freight Rates and the
Real Cost of Transportation
The essential difference between Soviet and Canadian rates is that the latter contain the principle of charging "what the traffic will bear," whereas Soviet rates are conditioned by a combination of the desire to make rates match costs of providing service and the achievement of predetermined political ends. Under the force of public scrutiny, Canadian railways are beginning to base rates on the cost of providing service, but formulae for deriving this have only recently begun to gain practical acceptance by the railroads. Today, the chief factor which keeps Canadian freight rates down is the presence of actual or imagined competition, especially from trucks. Com-

petition between carriers is lacking in the USSR and rates which appear to favour one carrier over another (for example, water over rail, or trucks over rail), such as in the case of parallel rail-river hauls or short hauls, are determined by political and planning policy rather than by the free play of economic forces.

For many reasons, Canadian rate structures cannot serve as a reliable index of real transportation cost in assessing Soviet freight rates although pertinent comparison of the two provides some understanding of the degree and manner in which Soviet rates may deviate from real costs. Structural differences in the rate systems are also of considerable relevance in understanding differences in the factors which influence locational decisions and transportation flows in the two countries. There are many similarities between the rate structures, although there are also very noticeable differences. In some aspects, particularly for hauls over a long distance, and in rate preference for shipment of finished products rather than raw materials, Soviet rates are clearly adjusted to reinforce the overall planning objective of reducing both the size of shipments and the length of haul. The basis of Soviet rates is the cost of service, although, depending on planning policy, the entire rate, or parts of it on any item, may be higher or lower than the cost of service. There is little basis for concluding that Soviet rates provide a less meaningful measure of real transportation costs than Canadian rates. The published rate based on the cost of service is, therefore, a key item used by planners attempting to minimize transportation costs for a particular industry.

THE STRUCTURE OF
SOVIET FREIGHT RATES

Regional Differences in Rates
Railway systems in North America have used many rate-making devices to capture markets, to preserve initial advantages, and to obtain business, of which the most notorious was the American scheme using base points. In the United States, since the early 1920's, the Interstate Commerce Commission has been breaking up tariff schedules which are considered to be dis-

criminatory, i.e., which create or maintain an unfair advantage for certain areas.

In the USSR, the rate on any commodity for a given distance applies regardless of the points between which the distance is incurred. In Canada, rates are negotiated for every haul and a haul of the same length for the same good need not always cost the same amount of money. This results in a proliferation of rates, whereas in the Soviet Union the entire rate structure can be reproduced in a small manual.[2] In the USSR, preferential rates for particular hauls are used to stimulate action which normally would not arise from the application of standard rates. However, there are only 84 preferential tariffs—69 higher and 15 lower.[3] Consequently, most preferential rates are designed to encourage joint rail-water movement of given products. In particular it is intended that bulk goods should not move on a railway where that railway runs parallel to a river or canal system. A reduction of 30 per cent of the normal rail charge is accorded all goods if they include joint rail-water movement. Bulk freight moving parallel to waterways, in particular to the Volga, Kama, and Dneper rivers, the Moscow Canal, the Caspian, Black, and Azov seas, is subject to a higher tariff of 25-100 per cent.[4] In a North American situation, the railways would be forced to take cognizance of a waterway parallel to a railway because of potential competition, rather than from a desire on the part of the state or the railway to patronize that waterway.

Rate Differential on Processed
and Unprocessed Items

In Canadian rates, which include the concept of charging "what the market will bear," the value of an item is an indicator of how much the item can absorb in the way of transport charges before the price reaches a prohibitive level. A non-fragile item with a high value per unit weight can move a long distance before the cost of transportation seriously increases the delivered price. Such an item could move a long distance before the c.i.f. price was higher than the f.o.b. price of a local competing product at the market. Conversely, a bulky item of low value such as roundwood cannot be shipped very far before

[2]Arkhangel'skiy, comp., Spravochnik po Tarifam Zheleznodorozhnogo Transporta.
[3]S. F. Kuchurin, Tarify Zheleznykh Dorog SSSR, p. 92.
[4]Ibid.

transport charges assume a very high value relative to the
f. o. b. price. The problem facing all railways is that both
types of goods must be carried—low value and high value commodities. In Canada, the problem is partially resolved by
charging more per ton on the high-value item and less per ton
for carrying the low-value item. In some cases, the latter
may even be carried at a loss while a compensating profit is
taken on the transportation of the former. In the USSR, unless
modified by special considerations, policy is to relate the cost
of carrying both types of goods to the cost of providing the service.

Higher charges per unit weight on processed or semi-
processed commodities than on raw materials are important to
the location of processing facilities within any industry. The
industry analyzed in this study is characterized by major
losses of weight during processing. However, Soviet policy
is to set an identical rate per ton on related raw materials and
processed items thus encouraging the processing of weight-
losing raw materials before shipment. The same rate per ton
on roundwood and lumber reinforces the desirability of a raw
material location for sawmilling because the weight-loss in converting roundwood to lumber is 49 per cent. Thus, nearly
twice as much roundwood equivalent must be shipped as lumber, necessitating payment of twice as large transportation
charges.

A large differential between processed and unprocessed
items reduces the preference for moving only the former.
Selected rate differentials on raw materials and processed
items are shown in Table 30. In the USSR, the cost of shipping one ton of lumber and roundwood is the same. In Canada,
the cost of shipping roundwood is 20 per cent less than shipping lumber. There is still an advantage in shipping lumber
rather than roundwood but there is a greater likelihood that
the smaller advantage could be more easily offset by savings
in other inputs at the market. Thus, savings in other factors
assume a greater significance in pulling a weight-losing industry away from a raw-material location when the difference
in transport costs between shipping raw materials and processed products approaches the size of the weight-loss.

The material presented in Table 30 also shows that higher
transportation costs are placed on shipment of paper than on
lumber, and on paper than on roundwood. Although the care

97

TABLE 30. RELATIVE COST OF SHIPPING
RAW MATERIALS AND FINISHED PRODUCTS

Distance (Km's)	USSR Roundwood & Lumber As a Per Cent of Paper & All Pulp	Canada		
		Roundwood As a Per Cent of Lumber	Roundwood As a Per Cent of Paper	Lumber As a Per Cent of Paper
100	94	80	74	92
500	86	82	74	91
1000	73	82	75	92
1500	62	82	75	92
2000	62	82	74	91
2500	71			
3000	85			

SOURCE: Soviet costs derived from Arkhangel'skiy, comp., Spravochnik po Tarifam Zheleznodorozhnogo Transporta, Tables 19 and 24. Canadian costs derived from Canadian Pacific Railway class rates supplied by Mr. E. O. Riddell, Freight Rate Manager, CPR, Toronto, Ontario.

with which large rolls of newsprint, for example, must be handled to maintain the round form is greater than that accorded to shipment of lumber, the value of a ton of paper exceeds that of lumber and is, therefore, capable of absorbing a higher cost of transportation. Although it might be argued that the differential observed between lumber and paper in the USSR might be accounted for by a higher cost of service in transporting the latter, there is, in fact, a greater differential between shipment of lumber and paper in the USSR than in Canada.

In Canada, the differential between the two products is constant at 91-92 per cent, whereas it fluctuates considerably in the USSR between 94 and 62 per cent—a difference of 32 per cent. A steady relationship in the Canadian figures indicates that the taper of the rates is the same in each case, but that a higher differential is placed on commodities as their value increases relative to the basic processed item in any industry. In the Soviet case, the fluctuation can be attributed to differences in the taper of the two rates with distance.

The Taper of Freight
Rates with Distance

Freight rates in both Canada and the USSR decrease with increasing length of haul. Terminal costs are reduced proportionately with increasing distance and, although the actual cost of service probably is constant for each mile or kilometre of haul over uniform terrain, the rate structure on all items is tapered. Freight rate tapers are relevant to a study of location of the wood-processing industry because peculiarities in the taper affect the interregional flow patterns between areas of timber production, processing plants, and markets. Rates which constantly decrease with increases in distance reduce the penalty for long hauls or shipments to or from marginal areas. Rates which increase with distance are designed to curtail long hauls and to favour interrelationships between near or adjacent regions.

The taper in Soviet freight rates is based upon the concept of "normal length of haul" of any commodity. The normal haul is that distance which is considered by planners to be optimal for the commodity. The freight rate usually diminishes in step-like fashion until the normal length of haul is reached, at which time the rate may stay constant or it may begin to increase with further increases in movement. This concept is essentially circular in reasoning: the average length of movement of a commodity is measured, the rate structure correspondingly adjusted, further shipments occur which obviously should be affected by the "normal" haul and the structure is further adjusted. As a planning tool, however, this approach implies a logical economic structure which does not, in fact, exist. The length of haul of any commodity, if excessive, should become shorter as the concept is applied over a long period of time. In fact, the principle has not prevented a significant increase in the average length of haul of wood commodities (excluding fuelwood) over the past 25 years. The average length of haul of wood freight (excluding fuelwood) was 998 kilometres in 1950, 1274 km. in 1955, 1519 km. in 1960, and 1616 km. in 1965.[5] The average length of haul grew 27 per cent from 1955 to 1965, the period during which the current freight rates were in effect (the average length grew 58 per cent from 1940-1964, the period covered by this study). The increase in the length of haul has resulted from continuing eastward shifts in logging in response to growing markets and decreasing supplies of roundwood in the European parts of the USSR. Thus, although the average length of haul of wood freight corresponds

[5]Transport i Svyaz' SSSR, Statisticheskiy Sbornik, p. 103.

99

to the lower limit of the normal length of haul for roundwood (1501-2200 km.), the fact remains that Soviet authorities are displeased with the long hauls of wood freight which they appear to have reinforced by the freight rate structure (wood moves farther on the average than any other major commodity in the USSR). The average haul in the USSR appears excessive by Canadian standards and obviously reflects the impact on this mean figure of yet longer hauls.

The normal haul for items such as roundwood, lumber, plywood, pit-props, telegraph poles, and pulp wood in Soviet freight rates is 1501 to 2200 kilometres; for paper and paperboard, wood pulp, books and journals, the normal haul is 1501 to 3000 kilometres. In the former case, the rate begins to increase after 2200 kilometres, whereas in the latter case the rate remains the same after 3000 kilometres.[6] Thus, in the case of paper and related items, the normal length of haul must be considered any haul over 1501 kilometres although, by Canadian standards, the rate should continue to fall after 1501 kilometres if the planners were attempting to reduce the impact of distance on the supply of paper and such items to the market. Where the policy of setting a normal length of haul proves awkward and penalizes shipments to or from a distant area which planners using other criteria wish to encourage, the freight charges are covered by a special preferential tariff.[7] It must be noted that the length of haul might be equally long for lumber as for roundwood even if all processing occurred at the source of the raw material. Further analysis of this problem requires data on the composition of flows of wood freight in the USSR.

The taper of selected Soviet and Canadian freight rates, shown in Figure 11, decreases with an increase in distance in both countries until it reaches a mid-point or plateau. The Soviet rates cease to decline after reaching the point of normal length of haul; they tend to remain constant after that point or, as in the case of lumber and roundwood, to increase sharply after reaching this base level. The Canadian rate on lumber decreases in a very pronounced step-like fashion until reaching a minimum at 1200 miles. A step-like decrease in the Canadian rate on logs also occurs although the rate ceases to diminish after 1400 miles. It is interesting to note that the variation

---

[6]Arkhangel'skiy, comp., Spravochnik po Tarifam Zheleznodorozhnogo Transporta, Tables 19, 21, and 24.

[7]Kuchurin, Tarify Zheleznykh Dorog SSSR, pp. 73-74.

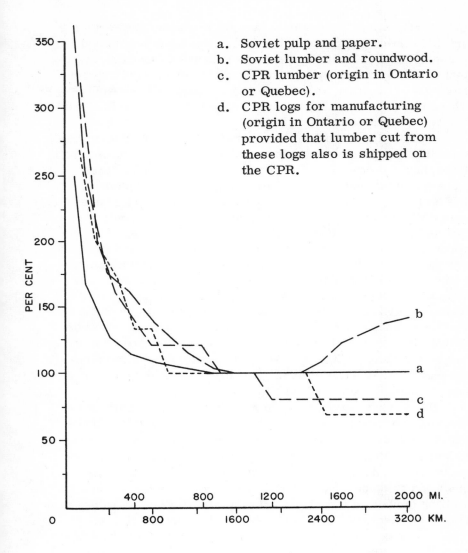

a. Soviet pulp and paper.
b. Soviet lumber and roundwood.
c. CPR lumber (origin in Ontario or Quebec).
d. CPR logs for manufacturing (origin in Ontario or Quebec) provided that lumber cut from these logs also is shipped on the CPR.

SOURCE: CPR data provided by Mr. E. O. Riddell, Freight Rate Manager, CPR, Toronto, Ontario. Soviet data derived from Arkhangel'skiy, comp., <u>Spravochnik po Tarifam Zheleznodorozhnogo Transporta</u>, Tables 19, 21, and 24

Figure 11. Variation in Freight Rates Per Ton-Kilometre or Ton-Mile (Per Cent of 1000-Mile or 1600-KM Rate)

in the rate on logs is less than the rate on lumber between 1100 and 1500 miles and greater than on lumber at several points between 200 and 500 miles. It may be concluded from Figure 11 that the structure of the taper in freight rates on similar commodities in the USSR and Canada is almost identical except where the Soviet rate begins to increase with distance in a manner designed to reduce long hauls.

Similarities and differences between the taper in Soviet and Canadian freight rates can also be measured by calculating the transportation cost per unit weight for various commodities and expressing that cost as a percentage of a base distance. In Figure 12, the total cost of transportation for each commodity with increasing distance was expressed as a percentage of the cost for 1,000 miles (1600·kilometres). The cost of transportation up to 1,000 miles is similar for all items but the cost curves diverge sharply after that distance. Soviet transportation costs are proportionately higher for long hauls than their Canadian counterparts. This is especially true when the cost increases artificially as on roundwood and lumber due to the desire to reduce long hauls. At this point the full significance of differences in the taper to the location of wood-processing can be evaluated. Figure 12 shows that after 2200 kilometres, the magnitude of savings to be gained from shipping paper and pulp instead of roundwood will increase sizeably.

The savings obtained by shipping lumber and paper instead of roundwood are presented in Table 31. The relationship between the cost of shipping lumber and its roundwood equivalent is steady at 49 per cent, although the magnitude of the saving becomes very large after 2000 kilometres. The size of the saving in shipping paper instead of roundwood is larger than that for lumber, although the relationship between the rates varies considerably. At 1500 and 2000 kilometres, for example, the saving obtained by shipping paper instead of roundwood drops to only 26 per cent and 25 per cent respectively; the influence of savings in consumption of other necessary inputs at the market (if this were the case) might be more effective at these points than at nearly all the other distances where the saving is approximately twice as large.

Fourteen examples have been drawn from Appendices E and F of shipments of lumber from raw-material oriented sawmills to the market (Table 32). Except where marked with an aster-

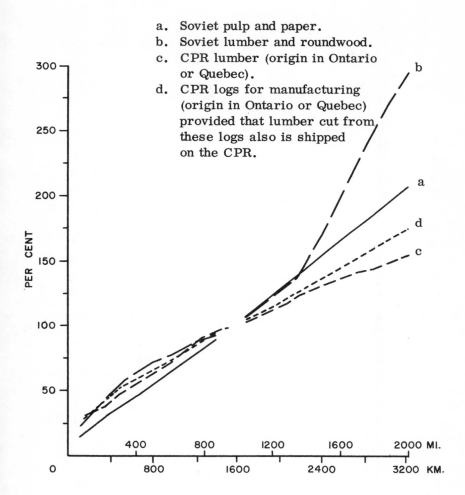

a. Soviet pulp and paper.
b. Soviet lumber and roundwood.
c. CPR lumber (origin in Ontario or Quebec).
d. CPR logs for manufacturing (origin in Ontario or Quebec) provided that lumber cut from these logs also is shipped on the CPR.

SOURCE: CPR data provided by Mr. E. O. Riddell, Freight Rate Manager, CPR, Toronto, Ontario. Soviet data derived from Arkhangel'skiy, comp., <u>Spravochnik po Tarifam Zheleznodorozhnogo Transporta</u>, Tables 19, 21, and 24.

Figure 12. Variation in Transportation Costs with Distance (Per Cent of 1000-Mile or 1600-Kilometre Cost)

TABLE 31. SAVING BY SHIPPING LUMBER AND
PAPER INSTEAD OF THEIR ROUNDWOOD EQUIVALENT

Distance	Lumber						Paper	
(Kilometres)	Saving/Ton of Roundwood Equivalent		Saving/M^3 of Roundwood Equivalent		Per Cent of f.o.b. Price/M^3 of Roundwood Equivalent		Saving/Ton of Roundwood Equivalent	
	Rubles	Per Cent	Rubles	Per Cent			Rubles	Per Cent
100	.84	49	.47	49	6.7		.96	51
200	1.14	49	.62	49	8.9		1.30	51
300	1.39	49	.76	49	10.9		1.50	48
400	1.70	49	.93	49	13.3		1.79	47
500	1.98	49	1.09	49	15.5		2.06	47
1000	2.89	49	1.59	49	22.8		2.45	38
1500	3.53	49	1.94	49	27.7		2.03	26
2000	4.63	49	2.55	49	36.5		2.60	25
3000	9.64	49	5.31	49	76.0		10.00	46
4000	13.50	49	7.42	49	106.0		14.70	48

SOURCE: Arkhangel'skiy, comp., Spravochnik po Tarifam Zheleznodorozhnogo Transporta, Tables 19 and 24.

isk, roundwood is also shipped. The difference between the cost of shipping lumber and its roundwood equivalent represents the saving in transport costs obtained by producing lumber at the raw material source. Higher transportation charges are incurred when roundwood instead of lumber is shipped between these origin-destination links.[8]

The possibility is raised that, although increases of distance bring about proportionate savings in transportation costs by shipping lumber and not roundwood, the actual saving per M^3 for relatively short distances (i.e., distances less than 1500-2000 kilometres) may not warrant the expenditure of scarce investment funds necessary to produce all required lumber in remote regions. It is feasible that Soviet authorities may choose to permit some lumber to be cut from roundwood imported from other regions if the differences in processing costs between the respective regions, and differences in the cost of shipping lumber and its roundwood requirement, are not too

[8]The argument here assumes that most of the demand for roundwood in unprocessed form is met from local supplies of roundwood. As some Soviet lumber is cut from roundwood imported from other regions, the point raised has considerable validity.

TABLE 32. DIFFERENTIAL IN TRANSPORTATION COSTS
BETWEEN LUMBER AND ITS ROUNDWOOD EQUIVALENT (Rubles)

Region of:			Transport Cost of:		
Origin	Destination	Distance (Km.)	Lumber 1M^3	Roundwood Equivalent	Difference
Northwest	Leningrad	1083	1.73	3.39	1.66
Northwest	Ukraine	1777	2.38	4.65	2.27
Upper Volga	Ukraine	1405	1.98	3.88	1.90
Upper Volga	Moldavia	2036	2.78	5.45	2.67
Volga-Vyatka	Ukraine	1523	2.10	4.13	2.03
Volga-Vyatka	N. Caucasus	2062	2.78	5.45	2.67
Krasnoyarsk	S. Urals	2186	2.92	5.74	2.82
Krasnoyarsk	Kazakhstan	2458	3.84	7.55	3.71
E. Siberia	Kuzbass	2608	4.52	8.86	4.34
E. Siberia	Central Asia	4990	9.94	19.50	9.56
Khabarovsk	C.B.E.*	7952	16.54	32.40	15.86
Khabarovsk	Azerbaydzhan*	9020	18.72	36.78	18.06
Far East	Mid-Volga*	7448	15.26	30.00	14.74
Far East	North East	1219	1.84	3.60	1.76

*Roundwood is not shipped between these regions.

NOTES: The origin-destination links appear in the actual shipment pattern (Appendix E) and the optimum pattern (Appendix F).

Transportation costs were calculated from Arkhangel'skiy, comp., Spravochnik po Tarifam Zheleznodorozhnogo Transporta, Table 19. The cost of shipping 1 ton of lumber and roundwood is the same. However, due to a different weight per unit volume (i.e., per M^3), the cost of shipping 1 M^3 of lumber is less than that of shipping 1 M^3 of roundwood. Thus, 1 M^3 of lumber weighs .55 metric tons while 1 M^3 of roundwood weighs .7 metric tons. Roundwood weighs 27.3 per cent more per M^3 than lumber (roundwood contains moisture which is removed from lumber during the drying process). The cost per M^3 of shipping roundwood is 27.3 per cent greater than that of shipping 1 M^3 of lumber. Production of 1 M^3 of lumber requires 1.54 M^3 (r). The cost of shipping the amount of roundwood equivalent of 1 M^3 of lumber, therefore, is 1.96 (i.e., 1.54 x 1.273) greater than shipping lumber. The saving achieved in all examples by shipping lumber instead of its roundwood equivalent is 49 per cent.

large. Thus, given national investment priorities, Soviet planners may decide to permit shipment on a short-term basis out of northern and eastern regions for processing in established areas, thereby saving the cost of providing additional social services, amenities, and infrastructure in relatively inhospitable and expensive areas. The Soviet practice of permitting rates to decrease until reaching the distance set as the normal length of haul appears to ensure that the magnitude of the difference between shipping lumber and its roundwood requirement will stay within manageable proportions up to and including the normal length of haul. In Table 32, shipments of roundwood do not occur between those origins and destinations which register the largest saving by shipping lumber. The distances between these origins and destinations exceed the normal length of haul. The large saving achieved in these cases by shipping lumber only seems to outweigh any savings in capital investment, etc., which could be achieved by locating production in traditional regions.

Transportation Costs
and Commodity Prices

It was demonstrated in the foregoing section that weight-loss and rate structure largely determine whether raw materials or finished products will be shipped. In fact, these two features can play a large role in the wood-processing industries in determining whether processing is oriented toward the source of the raw materials or toward the market. A third factor, that of the relationship between transportation costs and the value of an item, also has significance in assessing the relative abilities of raw materials and finished products to move long distances. Roundwood is less able to bear long transport hauls than lumber because at any distance transport costs assume a larger proportion in the f.o.b. price of roundwood than they do in lumber (Figure 13). In a market economy, purchasers of roundwood should be more conscious of alternate sources of roundwood and of alternate (substitute) kinds of raw materials than purchasers of lumber.

The greater importance of transportation costs to roundwood than to lumber also has significance to the distance at which the markets for both can be located away from the source of supply. Because transportation costs assume a greater value, relative to the f.o.b. price, more quickly on roundwood than they do on lumber, the market for roundwood in unprocessed form should be closer to the source of supply (i.e., the friction of distance is greater) than the market for lumber. The larger the transport costs, relative to the f.o.b. price of a commodity, therefore, the smaller the distance which that commodity should be shipped to its market. The saving in shipping lumber instead of its roundwood equivalent is considerable when expressed as a percentage of the f.o.b. price of the roundwood equivalent (Table 31). The saving is appreciable beyond the normal length of haul (i.e., beyond 2200 km.).

The examples in Table 33 (the origin-destination links are the same as those in Table 32) demonstrate that transport costs are much greater in the f.o.b. price of roundwood than for lum-

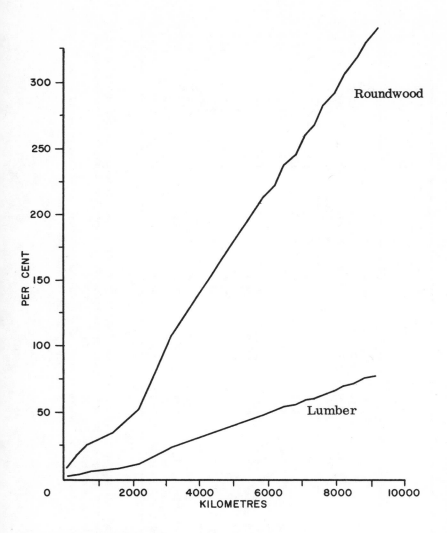

NOTE: An average Soviet price of $1M^3$ of roundwood (coniferous) is based on a production cost of R7.00/M^3 cited in Vasil'yev and Zheludkov, "Problemy Uluchsheniya Otraslevoy Struktury i Razmeshcheniya Lesnoy Promyshlennosti, " p. 402. An average Soviet price of $1M^3$ of lumber (coniferous) is based on production costs of R24.34 cited in P. E. Titkov, and S. I. Kantor, "Transport i Spetsializatsiya Proizvodstva, " Lesnaya Promyshlennost', p. 26 (cost for a mill cutting 125,000 M^3 of lumber annually).

Figure 13.   Transport Costs as a Per Cent of Production Costs

TABLE 33. THE RELATIONSHIP BETWEEN TRANSPORT
COSTS AND THE PRICE OF A COMMODITY (Rubles)

| Region of: | | 1 M³ of Roundwood | | | | | 1 M³ of Lumber | | |
Origin	Destination	(1) Price f.o.b. Origin	(2) Price f.o.b. Origin+ Total Cost	(3) Price of Local Roundwood in Region of Destination	(4) Transport Cost as a Per Cent of (1)	(5) Excess of Delivered Price Over Local Price	(6) Price f.o.b. Origin[c]	(7) Price f.o.b. Origin+ Transport Cost	(8) Transport Cost as a Per Cent of (6)
Northwest	Leningrad	6.49	8.69	6.60	33.9	2.09	24.34	26.07	7.1
Northwest	Ukraine	6.49	9.51	9.42	46.5	.09	24.34	26.72	9.8
Upper Volga	Ukraine	6.45	8.97	9.42	39.1	-.45	24.34	26.32	8.1
Upper Volga	Moldavia	6.45	9.99	7.40	54.9	2.59	24.34	27.12	11.4
Volga–Vyatka	Ukraine	6.45	9.13	9.42	41.6	-.29	24.34	26.44	8.6
Volga–Vyatka	N. Caucasus	6.45	9.99	6.77b	54.9	3.22	24.34	27.12	11.4
Krasnoyarsk	S. Urals	6.12	9.84	8.18	60.8	1.66	24.34	27.26	12.0
Krasnoyarsk	Kazakhstan	6.12	11.01	14.58	79.9	-3.57	24.34	28.18	15.8
E. Siberia	Kuzbass	5.99	11.74	9.14	96.0	2.60	24.34	28.86	18.6
E. Siberia	Central Asia	5.99	18.64	14.58	211.2	4.06	24.34	34.28	40.8
Khabarovsk	C.B.E.	8.63	29.69	6.77b	244.0	22.92	24.34	40.88	70.0
Khabarovsk	Azerbaydzhan	8.63	32.45	14.36a	276.0	18.09	24.34	43.06	76.9
Far East	Mid-Volga	11.56	30.98	6.77b	170.0	24.21	24.34	39.60	62.7
Far East	North East	11.56	13.90	7.27	20.2	6.63	24.34	26.18	7.6

aFigure for Georgia.

bRegional price not available. Average price for RSFSR of R6.77 is used, although the real price would probably exceed this figure. Price of roundwood for all regions derived from Vasil'yev and Zheludkov, "Problemy Uluchsheniya Otraslevoy Struktury i
Razmeshcheniya Lesnoy Promyshlennosti, " p. 402.

cPrices for lumber are not available. Average price of 1 M³ of coniferous lumber was derived from Titkov and Kantor, "Transport i Spetsializatsiya Proizvodstva, " p. 26 (prices at a mill cutting 125,000 M of lumber annually).

ber shipped the same distance. Although competitors are not able to take advantage of such a situation in the USSR, Table 33 does reveal the very large expenditures made on shipping both roundwood and lumber.

In fact, Table 33 also demonstrates how the Soviet manner of setting prices does not bring about a spatial price equilibrium such as the theoretical equilibria shown in Appendices A, C, D, and F. Most Soviet shipments of roundwood appear to arrive at their destinations with a greater c.i.f. price than the f.o.b. price for local roundwood. From the examples given here, it appears that Soviet prices do not serve as indicators of regional allocation of raw materials or finished goods. The prices appear to be accounting devices rather than regulators of supply and demand. The discrepancies shown in Table 33, however, reinforce the assumption made in the present study that Soviet freight rates serve as very important indicators for planning interregional movements of raw materials and processed goods.

VII

Conclusions

The purpose of this investigation has been to analyze transport costs as a factor in the location and flow patterns of the Soviet wood-processing industry. Although the role of transport costs in the spatial organization of the wood-processing industry has been given particular attention, the analysis has relevance to the general problem of the structure and influence of transport costs in industrial location per se. Toward an understanding of the general problem, this study has attempted to evaluate the relationship between freight rate structure, weight-loss and the value of a commodity, and the location of a major processing industry. Although these relationships have been examined within the context of the Soviet wood-processing industry, the conclusions drawn and the methods employed may have considerable relevance to the wood-processing industry in all countries.

ANALYTICAL TECHNIQUES:
AN EVALUATION

The techniques used to analyze a problem contribute directly to the manner in which it is solved. Use of basic and aggregated regional units has facilitated combination and rearrangement of data to obtain an aggregate representation for the entire wood-processing industry and to permit a concise areal representation of all data. Use of a consistent system of regions is the first step in application of conversion factors which relate the production of any branch of an industry to a uniform base for comparison with all other branches of that industry.

Data in this study have been presented in comparable terms for all branches of the wood-processing industry and an aggregate total figure of production has been derived in each region. This served as a basis for calculation and evaluation of optimal flow patterns of roundwood and lumber between regions.

The degree of spatial association between wood-processing (including its major component branches) and related phenomena has been measured by coefficients of correlation and of geographic association. These techniques were used to describe the degree of locational orientation of the wood-processing industry toward a raw-material location in 1964. The coefficient of geographic association was employed to show that practically no changes have occurred in the locational orientation of wood-processing between the years 1940, 1956, 1960 and 1964. During this period, lumber has maintained a high raw-material orientation while pulp and paper have consistently shown an indifferent orientation to either the raw material (roundwood) or the market (population). The orientation of pulp and paper production is difficult to assess with these coefficients because it is concentrated spatially. Even if it were completely oriented towards the source of raw materials, this spatial concentration in several of the regions of wood surplus would lead to a low value for either coefficient. Because very little of the total Soviet roundwood is consumed by the pulp and paper industry, plants could be located in a market region and consume a combination of local roundwood and substitutes for roundwood, such as waste paper. Lumber production, on the other hand, is not spatially concentrated and consumes a very large share of the national production of roundwood. Coefficients derived by these techniques are a basis for understanding the significance of the pattern of interregional flows of roundwood and finished products, and the importance of weight-loss during processing to the location of industry.

It is difficult to envisage evaluation of the type and size of flow patterns presented in this study without the application of linear programming techniques and the availability of a high-capacity electronic computer. The Transportation Problem, one formulation of the general linear programming approach, permits the optimum pattern of flows between regions of supply and demand to be determined. The primary solution to this problem presents a pattern of flows with a minimal aggregate cost of transportation while a secondary solution, the "dual," provides a system of spatial equilibrium prices, both f.o.b. and c.i.f., for the commodity being analyzed. Comparison of actual and theoretical flow patterns shows that the major actual flow patterns correspond in orientation with the theoretical pattern. It may be concluded that the Soviet planning apparatus is capable of achieving an economic distribution of major shipments of roundwood and lumber between regions based on the desire to minimize transportation costs. The aggregate pattern of actual flows, however, does not correspond with the theoretical pattern because of numerous small shipments in the form of back and cross hauls. It is suggested that most of the distortions to the optimum pattern of flows by small shipments may be caused by significant differences in the grade or quality of the commodity being shipped.

LOCATIONAL ORIENTATION OF THE SOVIET WOOD-PROCESSING INDUSTRY

The most economic location pattern of the wood-processing industry in terms of savings in transport costs is that which corresponds to the distribution of the raw material—roundwood. The large weight-loss during the conversion of roundwood into lumber, pulp, and paper, coupled with the resulting differential in transport cost in shipment of finished goods instead of roundwood, appear to influence strongly the orientation of wood-processing industries toward a location at the source of the raw materials. The relationship of transport costs to the price of a commodity shows that lumber can move greater distances than roundwood before transport costs become disproportionately large relative to the f.o.b. price of the commodity. Transport costs, therefore, both in relation to the weight-loss during processing and as a percentage of the f.o.b. price of a commodity, clearly favour the shipment of lumber, pulp, and paper instead of roundwood, and create a greater friction of distance in the transportation of raw materials than on finished products.

A large differential between the cost per unit weight of moving roundwood and finished products favours a location at the source of the raw materials. A small differential provides a greater opportunity for savings in other expenditures to influence the location of processing. Thus, in an industry where the differential on raw materials and finished products was minor, factors other than transport costs would play a significant role in determining the location of production. In wood-processing, however, the differential is always sufficiently great that other costs do not appear to act as major influences in location. Soviet wood-processing industries, however, are not completely oriented toward the source of the raw materials and, consequently, some other factors must occasionally influence location. The political and administrative changes (especially since 1940) in the areas now encompassed by the USSR have disrupted the market and raw-material patterns of a significant portion of the Soviet pulp and paper industry. Wartime disruption of plant capacity and construction plans is also probably reflected in the contemporary orientation of these processing plants. The supply of some types of pulp to various paper mills may influence the location of both the pulp and paper mills just as the integration of sawmills and consumers of wood chips might deflect the orientation of some pulp plants away from a strict orientation to the source of roundwood. The patterns shown in this study are analyzed by railway transport costs which clearly favour a raw-material location of processing. It is possible, however, that some of the Soviet wood-processing industry assembles raw, materials by water and that the resulting savings permit a location of processing closer to the market than to the raw material. The structure of costs on waterborne shipments, and the policy of Soviet planners toward water transportation of commodities, have not been analyzed in this study but it is felt that they may affect the location of the wood-processing industry in some cases.

FLOW PATTERNS

Interregional shipments of roundwood and lumber comprise about one-quarter of the total Soviet production of each item. Some of the roundwood shipped is consumed in unprocessed form while the rest is destined for processing. The major flows of both commodities correspond to an optimal pattern based on minimum transport costs, thereby confirming the major hypothesis of this study. Many small shipments which do not correspond to the optimal pattern probably reflect qualitative differences in the commodity being shipped. Refinements in the actual and theoretical flow data to include a breakdown of regional supply and demand by grade and species of roundwood and lumber would permit evaluation of the extent to which the total actual flow pattern corresponded to the optimal pattern. Unfortunately, at the present time such data are not available.

THE LOCATIONAL SIGNIFICANCE OF THE STRUCTURE OF SOVIET FREIGHT RATES

Soviet freight rates favour a raw-material location for wood-processing because they are the same per ton on lumber as on roundwood and are only slightly higher on pulp, paper, and paperboard than on roundwood. The weight-loss during processing of roundwood into these items results in a large differential between the cost·of shipping raw materials and finished products. The same sort of relationship exists in Canada although the differential is slightly less. The magnitude of savings in transport costs by shipping the finished product instead of roundwood increases with distance and further enhances orientation toward the source of raw materials. The Soviet rate on roundwood and lumber increases significantly after 2200 kilometres, thus increasing even more the magnitude of savings achieved by shipment of lumber. The rate on pulp, paper, and paperboard remains constant after 1500 kilometres thus creating a still larger difference in the cost of shipping raw materials and finished goods. Except for the increase in the rate on roundwood and lumber after the "normal length of haul," Soviet rates appear to be equally representative of the costs of transportation as their Canadian counterparts.

SCOPE FOR FURTHER RESEARCH

Many aspects of industrial location are touched upon in this study which appear to require further scrutiny and investigation.

The use of conversion factors to reduce all physical output to a common denominator suggests that this technique could be used in other studies to generate or estimate data to permit application of other criteria of measurement. The same approach might be applied to the Canadian wood-processing industry or to other processing industries in the USSR.

It has been assumed that the species of all shipments of roundwood and lumber are of equal utility and that any species may be substituted for any other species. Future studies of the wood-processing industry should attempt to obtain sufficient data to obviate the need for such an assumption and to examine the consequent increase in precision. Greater differentiation in the quality of commodities might explain the chaotic nature of the present interregional pattern of small shipments.

It has been established here that there is a need to attempt further linear programming analysis in which transport costs are combined with costs of production and market prices to assess the efficiency of the present regional location of wood-processing. In other words, in the present study the locations and size of supply and demand are given and optimal flows are calculated. Another problem would be to calculate the optimal location of supply and demand. Several refinements could, therefore, be made. The approach used here could be applied to determine, for example, the optimal pattern of logging. The distribution of logging has not been thoroughly evaluated in this study and the location of logging has been accepted as the source of the raw material. Having obtained the optimal pattern of logging, it would be possible to analyze further the pattern of flows between the source of the raw material and the wood-processing industry. The location of wood-processing also has been accepted as given. Research could focus on the optimal location of wood-processing plants once sufficient data were obtained.

The structure of wood-processing and other industries in various regions are not investigated in this study. Now that the patterns of location on a national level have been established, useful studies could be done to analyze the organization of location and material flows within some of the larger regions of the USSR and the relationship which wood-processing has to other industries at various stages in Soviet development.

The overwhelming need in future studies is to maintain the universality of approach which is attempted here. In the past,

115

studies of Soviet industrial development have tended to view Soviet geography and location policy strictly within the context of the USSR. Very few attempts have been made to view the processes at work in the USSR as the same kind of processes which are at work in other industrial societies. The Soviet Union has been thought of often as unique and the problems of its geography as peculiar to a Marxist form of government. Not only are there other Marxist governments in Europe, but also the time has come to view the economic geography of the USSR as part of economic geography per se. Consequently, for useful comparative purposes, future studies should be organized to ask the same questions, to use the same statistical techniques, and to approach the topic in the same organizational manner as in the West.

Appendices

Appendix A

OPTIMUM SHIPMENT OF ROUNDWOOD BETWEEN OBLASTS, KRAYS AND AUTONOMOUS REPUBLICS, 1964 (M³ x 10⁶)

FROM \ TO	Leningrad	Moscow	Yaroslavl	Vladimir	Ivanovo	Kaluga	Ryazan	Tula	Tatar	Mari	Mordovian	Chuvash	Rostov	Orenburg	Kalmyk	Chelyabinsk	Omsk	Novosibirsk	Altay	Kemerovo	Magadan	Krasnodar	Stavropol	Dagestan	Kabardinian-Balk	North Osetian	Chechen-Ingush	Ulyanovsk	Bashkir
Murmansk	1,243																												
Karelia		5,623																											
Novgorod															93							636	861						
Vologda			384																						157				
Archangel	1,609																												
Komi																													
Kalinin													2,990																
Kostroma					82																								
Gorki				185	53																			337		130	218		
Kirov						161	221	3,198																					
Udmurt																												16	
Perm									1,109	361	53	331		767															464
Sverdlovsk																													
Tyumen																													
Kurgan																													
Tomsk																914													
Krasnoyarsk																	505	592	61	2,101									
Irkutsk																				1,408									
Chita																													
Tuva																													
Buryat																													
Maritime																													
Khabarovsk																													
Amur																		321											
Sakhalin																					24								
Yakut																													
Smolensk																													
Pskov																													
Total Consumption	2,852	5,623	384	185	135	161	221	3,198	1,109	361	53	331	2,990	767	93	914	505	913	61	3,509	24	636	861	337	157	130	215	16	464
Delivered Value Rubles/M³	23.6	23.4	23.1	23.3	23.7	23.7	23.7	23.7	22.6	22.7	23.0	22.7	25.6	22.4	26.1	19.3	16.8	15.7	16.1	15.7	1.1	26.1	26.1	26.6	27.0	27.0	26.4	22.9	21.1

118

Region	Belgorod	Voronezh	Kursk	Orel	Bryansk	Lipetsk	Tambov	Penza	Astrakhan	Volgograd	Kuybyshev	Saratov	Ukraine	Moldavia	Estonia	Latvia	Lithuania	Kalinin-grad	Byeloru-ssia	Georgia	Azerbáyd-zhan	Armenia	Kazakhstan	Turkestan	Tadzhiki-stan	Kirgizia	Uzbekistan	Total Supply	Prices f.o.b. Rubles /M
Murmansk															314													314	21.5
Karelia													777		539	262	1,353	1,514	1,815									7,503	22.0
Novgorod														776														776	22.9
Vologda													3,673	610						400								6,430	22.6
Archangel													6,487															6,487	22.0
Komi													7,330															7,978	20.7
Kalinin																				392								392	23.9
Kostroma																												392	22.5
Gorki	394	873	362	281	427	360	265	51					854															3,844	23.4
Kirov																					139							139	22.0
Udmurt																					383							7,724	22.6
Penza																					779							850	21.0
Sverdlovsk										2,324		1,537	3,136									644	4,606					9,642	20.7
Tyumen									1,081		879												1,630					6,287	20.3
Kurgan																												2,696	20.5
Tomsk											63																	63	17.1
Krasnoyarsk											156															371		3,232	15.6
Irkutsk																				561								5,520	13.1
Chita																											2,779	6,956	9.4
Tuva																									286			676	16.8
Buryat																							32					32	11.6
Maritime																								60	520			1,408	2.2
Khabarovsk																								98				98	3.0
Amur																										652		652	3.0
Sakhalin																								220				220	0.0
Yakut																								127		11		131	12.5
Smolensk																				169								169	24.3
Pskov															139													139	23.2
Total Consumption	394	873	362	281	427	360	265	51	1,081	2,324	1,098	1,537	22,257	1,386	853	401	1,353	1,514	1,815	1,522	1,301	644	6,268	505	806	1,034	2,779	80,699	
Delivered Value Rubles/m³	24.7	24.2	24.3	24.1	24.1	24.0	23.8	23.2	24.6	24.2	22.9	23.3	25.1	25.9	24.1	24.3	24.5	24.7	24.5	29.2	28.3	30.3	20.5	27.1	27.1	22.4	23.5		

Appendix B

ACTUAL INTERREGIONAL MOVEMENT OF ROUNDWOOD, 1964

(M³ x 10³)

TO \ FROM	1	2	3	4	5	6	7	8	9	10	11	12	13	14	15	16	17	18
Northwest	27,712.2	282.1	16.2	896.9	123.9	0.2	26.2	163.1	0.8	0.0	0.0	0.0	1.7	9.4	1.6	0.0	0.0	0.0
Leningrad	1,947.6	14,851.7	7.0	2.8	36.1	1.0	94.6	312.6	0.1	0.0	0.0	0.0	6.4	106.5	79.0	0.0	0.0	0.0
Murmansk	272.8	0.1	1,477.1	0.8	0.0	0.0	0.3	1.3	0.2	2.1	0.0	0.0	0.0	0.5	495.3	0.1	0.1	0.0
Komi	3.7	0.0	0.0	4,678.5	0.3	0.3	0.3	632.7	0.1	0.0	1.0	0.0	3.4	11.7	11.5	0.1	0.0	0.0
Moscow	1,581.2	1,163.0	0.0	386.5	4,458.5	6.0	1,278.3	832.7	12.4	3.4	0.0	0.0	7.9	2.6	36.0	0.0	0.0	0.0
Prioka	1,131.9	201.4	0.0	690.1	67.4	1,715.8	327.3	285.8	2.8	0.0	0.0	0.0	26.2	5.4	179.4	2.9	0.7	0.0
Upper Volga	260.6	161.9	0.0	76.8	26.1	0.3	6,710.9	16,214.5	0.1	0.0	32.2	0.0	1.1	270.1	134.7	0.3	0.3	0.0
Volga-Vyatka	163.8	62.8	0.1	1.1	8.5	32.4	1,581.9	505.1	5.0	20.3	11.9	0.0	2.9	74.9	430.4	58.2	22.6	0.0
C.B.E.	289.2	140.6	0.1	269.0	26.4	0.0	67.6	748.9	709.9	1.8	3.0	144.7	16.5	1,574.4	186.8	13.4	12.3	0.0
Mid-Volga	0.6	4.5	0.1	0.0	4.1	0.0	43.4	92.3	4.4	4,079.4	0.0	0.0	0.7	1,372.4	63.2	1.6	3.0	0.0
Volga-Littoral	9.9	0.0	0.1	1.7	0.1	1.3	8.4	132.1	19.3	210.5	2,094.9	0.0	0.0	2,973.9	580.3	23.6	28.6	0.0
Lower Volga	1.5	0.5	0.0	0.1	0.3	0.2	14.0	566.0	0.3	3.2	5.4	115.5	0.0	14,182.3	92.8	6.9	0.1	0.0
North Caucasus	82.2	28.9	0.0	34.8	0.1	0.0	118.4	40.7	0.2	194.9	28.7	395.1	4,298.6	8.1	17,474.9	164.3	6.9	0.0
W. Urals	0.0	0.0	0.0	0.0	0.0	0.0	0.0	0.2	0.2	0.1	0.0	0.0	1.1	399.1	726.3	295.5	0.0	0.0
Mid-Urals	0.0	0.0	0.0	1.4	0.0	0.6	0.0	257.5	0.6	0.0	0.0	0.0	0.2	0.0	228.4	290.7	0.0	0.0
S. Urals	0.0	0.0	0.0	0.0	0.2	0.0	0.0	0.0	0.0	84.2	0.0	0.0	3.1	0.0	290.7	2,605.4	667.5	0.0
W. Siberia	0.0	0.0	0.0	0.0	0.0	0.0	0.0	0.0	0.0	0.0	0.0	0.0	1.5	0.0	0.1	0.0	6,202.8	6,211.3
Kurbass	0.0	0.0	0.0	0.0	0.0	0.0	0.0	0.0	0.0	0.3	0.0	0.0	0.5	0.0	0.0	0.0	0.0	0.0
Krasnoyarsk	0.7	0.0	0.0	0.0	0.0	0.0	0.0	0.0	0.0	0.0	0.0	0.0	0.2	0.0	0.0	0.0	0.0	0.0
E. Siberia	0.0	0.0	0.0	0.0	0.0	0.0	0.0	0.0	0.0	0.0	0.0	0.0	0.0	0.0	0.0	0.0	0.0	0.0
Khabarovsk	0.0	0.0	0.0	0.0	0.0	0.0	0.0	0.0	0.0	0.0	0.0	0.0	0.0	0.0	0.0	0.0	0.0	0.0
Far East	0.0	0.0	0.0	0.0	0.0	0.0	0.0	0.0	0.0	0.0	0.0	403.8	0.0	0.0	0.0	0.0	0.0	0.0
North East	8,528.5	935.0	147.0	2,218.6	165.4	31.6	741.9	2,222.1	4.4	383.0	22.8	22.8	21.9	1,291.5	1,734.5	0.0	0.0	0.0
Ukraine	778.3	209.7	130.4	0.0	15.5	2.5	24.2	39.4	1.1	0.0	2.1	0.0	2.3	1.3	0.2	0.0	0.0	0.0
Lith. & K'grad	482.9	77.6	3.0	1.6	2.0	12.6	70.0	64.7	0.0	0.0	0.0	2.1	0.1	0.2	0.0	0.0	0.0	0.0
Latvia	851.2	77.9	30.3	0.0	4.0	0.6	8.5	46.9	0.0	24.9	0.0	0.0	0.0	0.0	0.0	0.0	0.0	0.0
Estonia	1.5	0.0	0.0	2.3	0.0	0.0	0.0	56.8	0.0	0.0	14.6	392.4	2.6	74.3	156.2	0.0	0.0	0.0
Georgia	0.1	0.5	0.0	3.6	0.0	0.0	0.0	224.4	0.0	13.3	6.4	96.5	0.5	485.1	188.8	0.0	0.0	0.0
Azerbaydzhan	0.0	0.5	0.0	0.0	0.5	0.0	0.0	61.3	0.0	3.6	0.0	0.0	0.6	52.1	133.7	16.8	0.0	0.0
Armenia	0.0	0.0	0.0	0.0	0.0	0.0	0.0	4.5	0.0	42.5	1.4	0.0	1.4	58.0	142.9	4.0	0.0	17.1
Central Asia	0.0	0.0	0.0	0.0	0.0	0.0	0.0	9.0	0.2	0.0	42.5	0.0	0.0	70.6	1,545.8	9.0	99.0	201.6
Kazakhstan	223.3	2.0	0.0	0.0	431.2	0.0	71.6	19.2	0.0	0.0	0.0	0.0	0.0	13.9	0.7	184.7	230.9	0.0
Byelorussia	762.2	124.9	6.1	5.7	67.8	0.0	80.1	40.2	0.0	0.0	0.0	0.0	0.0	2.3	0.0	0.0	954.5	0.0
Moldavia	0.0	9.2	0.0	151.3	0.0	15.8	0.0	80.1	0.0	0.0	0.0	0.0	0.0	0.0	0.0	0.0	0.0	0.0
Total	45,085.7	18,334.5	1,817.4	9,423.3	5,438.0	1,821.5	11,267.6	23,372.1	763.1	5,067.5	2,224.4	1,663.1	4,409.8	23,598.7	24,931.0	3,282.6	8,326.0	6,430.1

FROM → / TO ↓	19	20	21	22	23	24	25	26	27	28	29	30	31	32	33	34	TOTAL
Northwest	3.1	0.0	3.1	0.0	0.0	0.0	0.0	0.0	0.0	0.0	0.0	0.0	0.0	0.0	12.6	0.0	29,253.0
Leningrad	0.0	0.0	1.6	0.0	0.0	0.0	0.0	0.0	0.0	0.0	0.0	0.0	0.0	0.0	1.4	0.0	17,448.4
Murmansk	13.1	0.0	0.2	0.0	0.0	0.0	0.0	0.0	0.0	0.0	0.0	0.0	0.0	0.0	0.6	0.0	1,767.0
Komi	0.0	0.0	0.7	0.0	0.0	0.0	0.0	0.0	0.0	0.0	0.0	0.0	0.0	0.0	0.0	0.0	5,180.0
Moscow	7.9	2.8	11.7	4.6	0.0	0.0	0.0	0.0	0.0	0.0	0.0	0.0	0.0	0.0	0.0	0.0	9,579.1
Priok	5.5	1.3	0.0	0.0	0.0	0.0	0.0	0.0	0.0	0.0	0.0	0.0	0.0	0.0	0.0	0.0	4,999.8
Upper Volga	0.1	17.8	0.0	0.0	0.0	0.0	0.0	0.0	0.0	0.0	0.0	0.0	0.0	0.0	0.0	0.0	7,572.7
Volga-Vyatka	0.6	0.2	3.1	0.3	0.0	0.0	0.0	0.0	0.0	0.0	0.0	0.0	0.0	0.0	8.8	0.0	18,632.5
C.B.E.	0.9	31.0	0.0	0.6	0.0	0.0	0.0	0.0	0.0	0.0	0.0	0.0	0.0	0.0	0.0	0.0	2,379.5
Mid-Volga	89.3	45.3	0.0	0.0	0.0	0.0	0.0	0.0	0.0	0.0	0.0	0.0	0.0	0.0	0.0	0.0	7,092.8
Volga-Littoral	55.5	8.7	0.0	0.0	0.0	0.0	0.0	0.0	0.0	0.0	0.0	0.0	0.0	0.0	0.0	0.0	4,141.6
Lower Volga	17.9	38.1	0.2	1.0	0.0	0.0	0.0	0.0	0.0	0.0	0.0	0.0	0.0	0.0	0.1	0.0	3,345.2
North Caucasus	92.4	0.6	2.1	0.2	0.0	0.0	0.0	0.0	0.0	0.0	0.0	0.0	0.0	0.0	0.0	0.0	7,072.0
W. Urals	1.5	16.3	0.0	0.0	0.0	0.0	0.0	0.0	0.0	0.0	0.0	0.0	0.0	0.0	0.0	0.0	14,319.3
Mid-Urals	2.5	349.2	0.2	0.7	0.0	0.0	0.0	0.0	0.0	0.0	0.0	0.0	0.0	0.0	0.0	0.0	17,807.2
S. Urals	481.5	360.0	0.0	1.7	0.0	0.0	0.0	0.0	0.0	0.0	0.0	0.0	0.0	0.0	0.0	0.0	5,072.3
W. Siberia	192.8	2,289.9	204.5	1.1	0.0	0.0	0.0	0.0	0.0	0.0	0.0	0.0	0.0	0.0	0.0	0.0	10,277.8
Kuzbass	606.3	64.0	74.6	3.6	0.0	0.0	0.0	0.0	0.0	0.0	0.0	0.0	0.0	0.0	0.0	0.0	12,717.7
Krasnoyarsk	12,651.6	0.0	0.0	0.0	0.3	0.0	0.0	0.0	0.0	0.0	0.0	0.0	0.0	0.0	0.0	0.0	17,422.9
E. Siberia	1.5	17,337.1	0.0	0.0	4.0	0.0	0.0	0.0	0.0	0.0	0.0	0.0	0.0	0.0	0.0	0.0	6,986.2
Khabarovsk	0.0	7.2	7,844.3	158.1	0.5	0.0	0.0	0.0	0.0	0.0	0.0	0.0	0.0	0.0	0.0	0.0	8,010.2
Far East	0.0	0.0	351.5	6,176.7	21.6	0.0	0.0	0.0	0.0	0.0	0.0	0.0	0.0	0.0	1.0	0.0	6,529.2
North East	0.0	0.0	13.5	13.5	1,947.6	0.0	0.0	0.0	0.0	0.0	0.0	0.0	0.0	0.0	0.0	0.0	1,994.7
Ukraine	181.7	0.0	0.9	0.0	0.0	11,266.6	0.0	0.0	0.0	0.0	0.0	0.0	0.0	0.0	106.4	0.0	30,435.4
Lith. & K'grad	0.0	0.0	0.3	0.0	0.0	0.0	1,272.7	31.7	0.0	0.0	0.0	0.0	0.0	0.0	90.9	0.0	2,572.0
Latvia	0.0	0.0	0.1	2.9	0.0	0.0	0.0	2,332.6	0.0	0.0	0.0	0.0	0.0	0.0	0.3	0.0	3,053.9
Estonia	0.0	0.0	0.2	0.3	0.0	0.0	0.0	0.0	817.3	0.0	0.0	0.0	0.0	0.0	0.9	0.0	1,837.9
Georgia	29.6	15.7	0.0	0.3	0.0	0.0	0.0	0.0	0.0	632.1	0.0	0.0	0.0	0.0	0.0	0.0	1,405.7
Azerbaydzhan	31.7	4.1	0.1	0.0	0.0	0.0	0.0	0.0	0.0	0.0	88.6	0.0	0.0	0.0	0.0	0.0	936.9
Armenia	23.0	0.6	0.0	0.0	0.0	0.0	0.0	0.0	0.0	0.0	0.0	73.6	0.0	0.0	0.0	0.0	492.6
Central Asia	1,094.0	1,708.7	0.0	0.0	0.0	0.0	0.0	0.0	0.0	0.0	0.0	0.0	23.2	0.0	0.0	0.0	3,383.0
Kazakhstan	545.8	1,707.2	0.0	0.0	0.0	0.0	0.0	0.0	0.0	0.0	0.0	0.0	0.0	1,514.4	0.0	0.0	6,780.9
Byelorussia	0.0	0.0	0.0	0.0	0.0	0.0	0.0	0.0	0.0	0.0	0.0	0.0	0.0	0.0	4,278.1	0.0	5,174.6
Moldavia	0.0	0.0	0.0	0.0	0.0	0.0	0.0	0.0	0.0	0.0	0.0	0.0	0.0	0.0	0.0	75.8	1,204.7
Total	16,129.8	24,005.8	8,512.7	6,365.6	1,974.0	11,266.6	1,272.7	2,364.3	817.3	632.1	88.6	73.6	23.2	1,514.4	4,501.2	75.8	276,874.0

Appendix C

OPTIMUM INTERREGIONAL SHIPMENT OF ROUNDWOOD, 1964

(M³ x 10³)

FROM \ TO	Moscow	Priokä	C.B.E.	Mid-Volga	Volga-Littoral	Lower Volga	North Caucasus	S. Urals	Kuzbass	Far East	North East	Ukraine	Lithuania & K'grad	Latvia	Estonia	Georgia	Azerbaydzhan	Armenia	Central Asia	Kazakhstan	Byelorussia	Moldavia	Total Supply	Prices f.o.b. Rubles/m³
Northwest												15,833											15,833	14.4
Leningrad													196	690									886	15.7
Murmansk													50										50	14.4
Komi	3,222														1,021								4,243	13.3
Upper Volga							2,662					1,513	1,053										3,695	15.0
Volga-Vyatka		2,602										37										1,129	4,740	14.8
W. Urals	919		1,617			1,682		1,790				1,786							816				9,279	13.4
Mid-Urals		576		2,025	1,917											774	848	419			673		7,124	12.4
W. Siberia																				1,340			1,340	12.7
Krasnoyarsk																				3,412			3,412	11.2
E. Siberia									3,843										2,544	196			6,583	6.0
Khabarovsk										164	21									318			503	0.0
Total Consumption	4,141	3,178	1,617	2,025	1,917	1,682	2,662	1,790	3,843	164	21	19,169	1,299	690	1,021	774	848	419	3,360	5,266	673	1,129	57,688	
Delivered Value Rubles/m³	15.9	16.1	16.6	14.5	15.0	16.6	18.3	13.9	11.7	2.2	2.5	17.5	17.6	17.2	16.8	20.5	19.2	22.2	18.6	16.1	17.2	18.5		

Appendix D

OPTIMUM SHIPMENT OF LUMBER BETWEEN OBLASTS, KRAYS AND AUTONOMOUS REPUBLICS, 1964 (M³ x 10³)

FROM	Moscow	Kaluga	Ryazan	Tula	Tatar	Mordovinian	Bashkir	Belgorod	Voronezh	Kursk	Orel	Bryansk	Lipetsk	Tambov	Penza	Kuybyshev	Saratov	Rostov	Orenburg	Kalmyk	Chelyabinsk	Kurgan	Novosibirsk	Krasnodar	Stavropol	Dagestan	Kabardinian-Balk	North Ossetian	Chechen-Ingush	Ukraine	Moldavia	Lithuania	Kaliningrad
Leningrad																														1,522	196	16	
Murmansk																														502			
Karelia																														1,004			
Novgorod																														472			
Vologda																														99			
Archangel	449							373																						105			
Komi										513																				6	78		
Yaroslavl																														45			
Vladimir																														101	609		
Ivanovo																														1,253			
Kalinin																														947			
Kostroma																														2,838			
Gorki																												148					
Kirov																				69					395								
Mari											288	20	388	103																			
Chuvash																		233															
Ulyanovsk																		70							96	507							
Udmurt																																	
Astrakhan																																	
Volgograd																		790												2,063			
Perm	1,828								724																								
Sverdlovsk		110	223	249																													
Tyumen														336	119				500														
Omsk							419																										
Tomsk																													294				
Altay					216											363					368												
Krasnoyarsk						127									95									378			145			294			
Irkutsk															51							33		112									
Chita																	250	15															
Tuva																																	
Kemerovo																																	
Buryat																																	
Maritime																																	
Khabarovsk																																	
Amur																																	
Sakhalin																							164										
Magadan																																	
Yakut																																	
Estonia																																74	119
Latvia																																207	
Total Consumption	2,277	110	223	249	216	127	419	373	724	513	288	20	388	439	265	363	250	1,108	500	69	368	33	164	490	491	507	145	148	294	10,977	883	297	119
Delivered Value Rubles/M³	19.3	19.5	19.4	19.5	18.0	18.8	16.3	20.3	20.0	22.0	19.8	19.8	19.7	19.5	18.8	18.0	18.8	21.2	17.3	21.6	14.8	14.6	12.1	21.4	21.6	17.6	21.7	21.7	21.4	21.0	21.6	20.6	20.7

	Smolensk	Pskov	Byelorussia	Georgia	Azerbaydzhan	Armenia	Kazakhstan	Turkestan	Tadzhikistan	Kirgizia	Uzbekistan	Total Supply	Prices f.o.b. Rubles /M³
Leningrad												196	19.2
Murmansk			519									519	18.1
Karelia			554									2,092	18.6
Novgorod												502	19.2
Vologda												1,004	19.0
Archangel												472	18.6
Komi	53											1,546	17.2
Yaroslavl		59										105	19.2
Vladimir												84	19.3
Ivanovo												45	19.2
Kalinin												710	19.3
Kostroma												1,253	19.0
Gorki												947	19.1
Kirov												2,838	18.6
Mari												612	18.9
Chuvash												233	19.1
Ulyanovsk												148	19.7
Udmurt					148							673	18.4
Astrakhan						198						198	21.7
Volgograd						362						362	21.4
Perm												2,083	17.8
Sverdlovsk												4,390	17.0
Tyumen												649	16.6
Omsk												119	15.9
Tomsk							213					1,225	13.1
Altay										93	15	15	14.4
Krasnoyarsk				1,409		133	2,417					4,069	11.9
Irkutsk											3,197	5,121	10.4
Chita												413	7.5
Tuva							60					60	12.8
Kemerovo										747		747	13.5
Buryat									252		723	975	8.7
Maritime								716				716	1.7
Khabarovsk					1,453							1,453	2.5
Amur									275			275	3.9
Sakhalin								4	378			382	0.0
Magadan					59	50					6	65	.8
Yakut												214	9.6
Estonia												193	19.2
Latvia												207	19.8
Total Consumption	53	59	1,073	1,409	1,660	743	2,690	720	905	840	3,941	37,930	
Delivered Value Rubles/M³	19.8	19.8	20.6	23.1	22.5	23.9	15.8	21.3	21.3	17.3	18.6		

125

Appendix E

ACTUAL INTERREGIONAL MOVEMENT OF LUMBER, 1964
(M³ × 10³)

FROM	1	2	3	4	5	6	7	8	9	10	11	12	13	14	15	16	17	18
Northwest	8,191.4	59.7	4.4	9.5	18.3	0.0	20.9	1.2	0.0	0.0	0.0	0.0	0.7	21.5	4.8	0.0	0.3	0.0
Leningrad	910.4	4,887.1	42.6	6.9	6.6	0.0	18.5	137.5	0.0	0.1	0.0	0.0	39.9	21.5	217.3	0.0	2.5	0.0
Murmansk	9.4	0.1	907.0	0.0	0.1	0.0	0.0	0.3	0.0	0.0	0.0	0.0	0.3	0.1	0.1	0.0	0.0	0.0
Komi	2.0	0.8	1.0	1,149.1	1.0	0.0	1.0	0.3	0.0	9.8	0.1	0.0	0.3	228.9	47.3	0.0	0.0	9.8
Moscow	657.7	165.2	0.0	251.1	4,734.1	2.5	406.2	606.9	0.0	0.3	0.1	0.0	82.5	49.5	50.6	0.0	19.0	6.3
Prioka	150.1	52.9	0.0	59.8	15.9	1,589.8	97.1	246.0	0.0	0.7	0.5	0.0	5.3	24.2	7.3	0.0	5.1	0.5
Upper Volga	42.8	8.0	0.0	28.9	0.5	0.0	2,635.0	40.9	0.0	7.6	0.9	0.0	41.3	92.8	33.4	0.0	9.0	0.9
Volga-Vyatka	1.8	5.7	0.0	1.3	0.3	0.0	3.3	5,608.0	0.0	2.5	0.5	0.1	8.5	153.5	445.7	0.0	5.1	14.2
C.B.E.	64.4	22.8	0.0	113.8	5.5	32.3	28.6	358.0	675.5	22.0	6.3	9.6	15.3	92.6	66.5	0.0	6.9	0.0
Mid-Volga	4.8	5.6	0.0	1.8	0.3	0.1	0.0	24.8	0.0	2,965.5	16.1	0.0	21.3	30.0	91.8	0.0	10.6	1.0
Volga-Littoral	18.9	3.8	0.0	0.0	9.1	0.0	0.0	57.5	0.0	16.7	1,756.4	0.0	6.9	55.1	34.3	0.0	7.6	1.7
Lower Volga	25.2	12.4	0.0	2.0	3.4	0.0	1.3	26.2	0.0	15.4	10.4	1,633.7	6.9	408.9	388.0	0.0	233.9	61.8
North Caucasus	0.1	18.8	0.0	0.7	2.9	0.0	25.6	279.1	0.0	83.3	106.8	390.5	2,633.9	6.9	10.8	5.5	0.3	0.0
W. Urals	0.0	0.3	0.0	0.0	0.0	0.0	0.0	0.8	0.0	0.0	0.0	0.0	8.5	3,354.0	12.0	0.0	4.7	9.1
Mid-Urals	0.1	0.0	0.0	0.0	0.0	0.0	0.0	0.1	0.0	0.0	0.0	0.0	8.1	12.0	5,278.7	0.0	52.1	16.3
S. Urals	0.4	0.0	0.0	0.0	0.0	0.0	0.0	7.2	0.0	58.3	12.5	0.0	2.0	17.1	221.9	2,046.4	123.5	0.0
W. Siberia	0.0	0.0	0.0	0.0	0.0	0.0	0.0	0.0	0.0	0.0	0.0	0.0	8.7	2.9	3.4	0.0	2,260.4	0.0
Kusbass	0.0	0.0	0.0	0.0	0.0	0.0	0.0	0.0	0.0	0.0	0.0	0.0	0.4	0.7	0.1	0.0	16.3	3,064.2
Krasnoyarsk	0.0	0.0	0.0	0.0	0.0	0.0	0.0	0.0	0.0	0.0	0.0	0.0	0.4	0.0	0.1	0.0	0.0	0.0
E. Siberia	0.0	0.0	0.0	0.0	0.0	0.0	0.0	0.0	0.0	0.0	0.0	0.0	0.4	0.0	0.0	0.0	0.0	0.0
Khabarovsk	0.0	0.0	0.0	0.0	0.0	0.0	0.0	0.0	0.0	0.0	0.0	0.0	0.0	0.0	0.1	0.0	0.0	0.0
Far East	0.0	0.0	0.0	0.0	0.0	0.0	0.0	0.0	0.0	0.0	0.0	0.0	0.4	0.0	0.0	0.0	0.0	0.0
North East	0.1	0.0	0.0	0.0	0.0	0.0	0.0	0.0	0.0	83.8	43.5	41.2	0.4	560.2	1,638.9	0.0	30.6	41.5
Ukraine	1,249.4	252.3	34.7	440.3	123.1	58.4	525.1	1,392.2	0.0	0.1	0.0	0.0	0.0	1.8	23.1	0.0	0.0	0.0
Lith. & K'grad	116.8	54.0	0.3	0.3	0.1	0.0	0.5	0.7	0.0	0.3	0.0	0.0	0.0	0.3	14.9	0.0	0.0	0.0
Latvia	84.6	27.5	12.3	0.0	0.0	0.0	0.0	0.4	0.0	12.0	0.1	14.3	0.5	23.1	0.5	0.0	46.9	0.0
Estonia	90.3	3.4	9.3	6.6	0.0	0.0	0.0	58.3	0.0	0.9	0.0	22.4	0.0	15.8	9.4	0.0	32.7	0.0
Georgia	2.2	0.1	0.0	1.4	0.0	0.0	2.1	67.9	0.0	7.2	0.0	33.2	0.0	3.4	6.4	0.0	5.5	9.5
Azerbaydzhan	1.0	0.1	0.0	0.0	0.0	0.0	0.0	33.1	0.0	64.7	1.8	0.0	4.3	30.4	14.1	0.0	171.7	41.7
Armenia	0.0	0.0	0.0	0.0	0.0	0.0	0.0	7.4	0.0	0.5	0.0	0.0	3.7	6.0	142.4	0.0	198.0	96.0
Central Asia	0.3	0.1	0.0	0.0	0.0	0.0	0.0	30.1	0.0	4.4	0.0	0.0	0.0	15.5	175.2	10.4	0.0	143.5
Kazakhstan	0.0	0.0	0.0	0.0	0.0	0.0	0.0	2.5	0.0	0.5	0.0	0.0	0.0	0.4	33.1	0.0	0.0	0.0
Byelorussia	367.4	43.5	0.0	4.2	0.5	0.0	3.3	16.8	0.0	0.0	0.0	0.0	0.0	0.0	7.6	0.0	0.0	0.0
Moldavia	219.4	40.3	96.1	0.9	18.9	0.0	41.7	0.0	0.0	0.0	0.0	0.0	0.0	0.0	0.0	0.0	0.0	0.0
TOTAL	12,318.0	5,664.4	1,106.6	2,078.7	4,939.3	1,683.4	3,810.3	9,009.4	675.4	3,333.9	1,961.5	2,145.2	2,904.7	5,225.9	8,969.6	2,062.3	3,226.9	3,518.0

	19	20	21	22	23	24	25	26	27	28	29	30	31	32	33	34	TOTAL
1 Northwest	5.5	0.0	0.0	0.7	0.0	0.1	0.0	0.0	1.0	0.0	0.0	0.0	0.0	0.0	24.8	0.0	8,364.8
2 Leningrad	3.4	0.0	0.0	0.0	0.0	2.6	0.0	0.0	0.0	0.0	0.0	0.0	0.0	0.0	7.4	0.0	6,304.5
3 Murmansk	6.6	0.0	0.0	0.0	0.0	0.0	0.0	0.0	0.0	0.0	0.0	0.0	0.0	0.0	2.3	0.0	924.0
4 Komi	0.0	0.0	0.0	0.0	0.0	0.0	0.0	0.0	0.0	0.0	0.0	0.0	0.0	0.0	0.0	0.0	1,153.5
5 Moscow	78.5	56.8	0.7	0.4	0.0	2.7	0.0	0.0	0.0	0.0	0.0	0.0	0.0	0.0	15.0	0.0	7,375.4
6 Prioka	12.9	6.9	0.0	0.0	0.0	0.3	0.0	0.0	0.0	0.0	0.0	0.0	0.0	0.0	0.4	0.0	2,349.2
7 Upper Volga	0.5	7.0	0.0	0.0	0.0	0.0	0.0	0.0	0.0	0.0	0.0	0.0	0.0	0.0	0.7	0.0	2,839.4
8 Volga-Vyatka	0.7	19.0	0.0	0.3	0.0	0.0	0.0	0.0	0.0	0.0	0.0	0.0	0.0	0.0	0.0	0.0	5,793.8
9 C.B.E.	19.2	0.0	0.0	0.0	0.0	0.0	0.0	0.0	0.0	0.0	0.0	0.0	0.0	0.0	0.4	0.0	2,047.9
10 Mid-Volga	75.2	236.1	3.0	9.4	0.0	1.8	0.0	0.0	0.0	0.0	0.0	0.0	0.0	0.0	0.5	0.0	3,505.0
11 Volga-Littoral	18.3	212.6	0.7	0.0	0.0	0.0	0.0	0.0	0.0	0.0	0.0	0.0	0.0	0.0	0.1	0.0	2,256.4
12 Lower Volga	12.5	131.0	0.0	0.0	0.0	0.0	0.0	0.0	0.0	0.0	0.0	0.0	0.0	0.0	0.0	0.0	1,960.8
13 North Caucasus	333.6	266.2	0.0	0.0	0.0	0.0	0.0	0.0	0.0	0.0	0.0	0.0	0.0	0.0	0.0	0.0	5,268.0
14 V. Urals	5.1	0.0	2.1	0.1	0.0	0.0	0.0	0.0	0.0	0.0	0.0	0.0	0.0	0.0	0.0	0.0	3,379.8
15 Mid-Urals	7.2	1.7	2.3	0.5	0.0	0.0	0.0	0.0	0.0	0.0	0.0	0.0	0.0	0.0	0.0	0.0	5,311.0
16 S. Urals	194.0	418.5	14.2	16.7	0.0	0.0	0.0	0.0	0.0	0.0	0.0	0.0	0.0	0.0	0.0	0.0	3,060.0
17 W. Siberia	24.6	104.2	64.9	31.2	0.4	0.1	0.0	0.0	0.0	0.0	0.0	0.0	0.0	0.0	0.0	0.0	2,493.9
18 Kuzbass	216.0	394.9	38.5	2.7	0.0	0.0	0.0	0.0	0.0	0.0	0.0	0.0	0.0	0.0	0.0	0.0	3,868.7
19 Krasnoyarsk	3,842.4	21.1	1.3	19.6	0.0	0.0	0.0	0.0	0.0	0.0	0.0	0.0	0.0	0.0	0.1	0.0	3,881.0
20 E. Siberia	3.4	3,833.0	24.2	13.7	0.0	0.1	0.0	0.0	0.0	0.0	0.0	0.0	0.0	0.0	0.1	0.0	1,950.7
21 Khabarovsk	0.0	5.1	1,931.9	24.2	0.0	0.0	0.0	0.0	0.0	0.0	0.0	0.0	0.0	0.0	0.0	0.0	2,142.0
22 Far East	0.0	0.1	49.5	2,092.4	0.0	0.0	0.0	0.0	0.0	0.0	0.0	0.0	0.0	0.0	0.0	0.0	837.4
23 North East	0.0	0.0	0.8	0.0	830.1	0.0	0.0	0.0	0.0	0.0	0.0	0.0	0.0	0.0	0.0	0.0	13,287.7
24 Ukraine	250.6	133.0	0.3	6.4	0.0	6,227.8	0.0	0.0	5.2	0.0	0.0	0.0	0.0	0.0	55.1	0.0	1,646.3
25 Lith. & K'grad	0.9	0.1	0.0	0.0	0.0	0.0	441.4	0.0	5.5	0.0	0.0	0.0	0.0	0.0	4.3	0.0	1,061.2
26 Latvia	5.5	0.0	0.0	0.0	0.0	0.0	0.0	903.9	0.0	0.0	0.0	0.0	0.0	0.0	2.6	0.0	684.7
27 Estonia	0.0	0.1	0.0	0.0	0.0	0.0	0.0	0.0	577.6	0.0	0.0	0.0	0.0	0.0	0.1	0.0	1,059.6
28 Georgia	297.4	8.1	0.4	0.0	0.0	1.7	0.0	0.0	0.0	545.6	0.0	0.0	0.0	0.0	0.0	0.0	958.6
29 Azerbaydzhan	273.9	8.7	0.1	0.0	0.0	0.0	0.0	0.0	0.0	0.0	517.6	0.0	0.0	0.0	0.0	0.0	476.6
30 Armenia	213.6	1,985.2	40.3	9.0	0.0	0.1	0.0	0.0	0.0	0.0	0.0	120.2	0.0	0.0	8.0	0.0	3,413.3
31 Central	325.9	879.9	75.2	7.6	0.0	0.1	0.0	0.0	0.0	0.0	0.0	0.0	551.7	0.0	0.0	0.0	4,837.4
32 Kazakhstan	310.2	1.2	451.4	50.5	0.0	0.0	0.0	0.0	0.0	0.0	0.0	0.0	0.0	2,510.6	1.4	0.0	2,479.7
33 Byelorussia	18.3	0.1	0.0	0.0	0.0	0.0	0.0	0.0	0.0	0.0	0.0	0.0	0.0	0.0	1,989.8	0.0	1,046.9
34 Moldavia	0.9	0.0	0.0	0.0	0.0	0.3	0.0	0.0	0.0	0.0	0.0	0.0	0.0	0.0	3.9	595.2	
	6,556.6	8,844.6	2,662.1	2,242.9	830.5	6,237.6	441.4	903.9	589.3	545.6	517.6	120.2	551.7	2,510.6	2,114.9	595.2	110,898.3

Total Shipped Between Regions: 26,692,480 м3

Appendix F

OPTIMUM INTERREGIONAL SHIPMENT OF LUMBER, 1964
(M³ x 10³)

FROM \ TO	Leningrad	Moscow	Priozka	C.B.E.	Mid-Volga	Volga-Littoral	N. Caucasus	S. Urals	Kuzbass	North East	Ukraine	Lith. & K'grad	Latvia	Estonia	Georgia	Azerbaydzhan	Armenia	Central Asia	Kazakhstan	Byelorussia	Moldavia	Total Supply	Prices f.o.b. Rubles/M³
Northwest											3,953											3,953	17.4
Murmansk												183										183	17.4
Komi	640											22	157	96						10		925	16.0
Upper Volga											519										452	971	17.8
Volga-Vyatka							2,128				1,087											3,215	17.7
Lower-Volga																	184					184	19.7
W. Urals											1,491									355		1,846	16.6
Mid-Urals		2,436	666	557																		3,659	14.9
W. Siberia					97														636			733	12.1
Krasnoyarsk				696		295													1,690			2,688	10.9
E. Siberia								998							514	441	150	2,861				4,964	6.9
Khabarovsk				120			235		363													711	2.2
Far East					74					7							20					101	0.0
Total Consumption	640	2,436	666	1,373	171	295	2,363	998	363	7	7,050	205	157	96	514	441	354	2,861	2,326	365	452	24,133	
Delivered Value Rubles/M³	18.4	17.7	17.8	18.7	15.3	16.4	20.4	13.8	11.5	1.8	19.8	19.9	19.2	18.8	21.8	20.9	22.2	16.9	14.8	19.5	20.6		

128

Bibliography

Abouchar, A. "Rationality in the Prewar Soviet Cement Industry." Soviet Studies, XIX (1967), 211-231.

Alexander, J. W. Economic Geography. Englewood Cliffs: Prentice-Hall, Inc., 1964.

Alonso, W. "Location Theory." Regional Development and Planning. Edited by J. Friedmann and W. Alonso. Cambridge: Massachusetts Institute of Technology, 1964.

Anderson, J. "Fodder and Livestock Production in the Ukraine: A Case Study of Soviet Agricultural Policy." The East Lakes Geographer, III (October, 1967), 29-46.

Arkhangel'skiy, A. S., compiler. Spravochnik po Tarifam Zheleznodorozhnogo Transporta. Moscow: Transzheldorizdat, 1955. (Reprinted, 1964.)

Atlas SSSR. Moscow: Glavnoye Upravleniye Geodezii i Kartografii, Ministerstvo Geologii i Okhrany Nedr SSSR, 1962.

Avrukh, A. Ya. Problemy Sebestoyimosti Elektricheskoy i Teplovoy Energy. Moscow: Energetika, 1966.

Balinski, M. L. and R. E. Gomory. "A Primal Method for the Assignment and Transportation Problems." Management Science, X (April, 1964), 578-593.

Baransky, N. N. Economic Geography of the USSR. Moscow: Foreign Languages Publishing House, 1956.

Barr, B. M. "The Role of Transfer Costs in the Location and Flow Patterns of the Soviet Wood-processing Industry." Unpublished Ph.D. dissertation, Department of Geography, University of Toronto, 1968.

Belousova, V. S., V. V. Glotov, and L. A. Kozlov. "Postanovka, Resheniye i Analiz Zadach Po Razmeshcheniyu i Spetsializatsii Otrasley Lesnoy Promyshlennosti." Modeli i Metody Optimal'nogo Razvitiya i Razmeshcheniya Proizvodstva. Nauchniye Trudy Novosibirskogo Universiteta, Seriya Ekonomika, Vypusk 3 (1965), 326-374.

Benenson, G. M., S. A. Obraztsov, and L. S. Bolyatinskaya. Perspektivy Razmeshcheniya Lesopil'no-Derevoobrabatyvayushchey Promyshlennosti. Moscow: G.L.B.I., 1960.

129

Birman, I. Ya. _Transportnaya Zadacha Lineynogo Programmirovaniya_. Moscow: Ekonomicheskaya Literatura, 1962.

Birman, I. Ya. and L. E. Mints. _Matematicheskiye Metody i Problemy Razmeshcheniya
Proizvodstva_. Moscow: Ekonomicheskaya Literatura, 1963.

Blalock, H. M., Jr. _Social Statistics_. New York: McGraw-Hill Book Co., Inc., 1960.

Bowles, W. D. "Economics of the Soviet Logging Industry." Unpublished Ph.D. dissertation. Columbia University, New York, 1957.

--------. "New Data on the Timber Industry of the USSR." _Journal of Forestry_, LVII,
No. 11 (1959), 822-824.

--------. "The Soviet Logging Industry—a Backward Branch of the Soviet Economy."
American Slavic and East European Review, No. 4 (1958), 426-438.

--------. "Understanding the Soviet Lumbering Industry." _Timber of Canada_, XIX, No.
11 (1958), 39-43.

Breyterman, A. D. _Ekonomicheskaya Geografiya SSSR_. Moscow: Vysshaya Shkola, 1965.

Bruce, R. W. _Interregional Competition in Lumber Markets of the Eleven Western States_.
Unpublished manuscript. Review Copy, Washington State University, 1968.

Bruk, I. S., ed. _Primeneniye Tsifrovykh Vychislitel'nykh Mashin v Ekonomike (Trans-
portnaya Zadacha Lineynogo Programmirovaniya)_. Moscow: AN SSSR, 1962.

Chisholm, M. _Geography and Economics_. Bell's Advanced Economic Geographies.
London: G. Bell and Sons Ltd., 1966.

Cole, J. P. and F. C. German. _A Geography of the USSR_. London: Butterworths, 1961.

Daggett, Stuart. _Principles of Inland Transportation_. 4th ed. New York: Harper and
Bros., 1955.

Dano, S. _Linear Programming in Industry, Theory and Applications_. Wien: Springer-
Verlag, 1965.

Dewdney, J. C. _A Geography of the Soviet Union_. London: Pergamon Press, 1965.

Dorfman, R., P. Samuelson, and R. Solow. _Linear Programming and Economic Analysis_.
New York: McGraw-Hill Book Co., Inc., 1958.

Duerr, W. A. _Fundamentals of Forestry Economics_. New York: McGraw-Hill, 1960.

Dzhalilov, Kh. I. _Problemy Syr'evoy Bazy Tsellyulozno-Bumazhnoy Promyshlennosti_.
2nd ed. Moscow: Lesnaya Promyshlennost', 1964.

Economic Commission for Europe, and Food and Agriculture Organization. Joint Working
Party on Forest and Forest Products Statistics. _Conversion Factors_. Fifth Session,
Geneva, 18-22 January, 1965.

Ekonomicheskaya Gazeta. No. 25, 1968.

Ekonomika i Matematicheskiye Metody, II, No. 2 (1966).

Feygin, Ya. G., chief ed. _Osobennosti i Faktory Razmeshcheniya Otrasley Narodnogo
Khozyaystva SSSR_. Moscow: AN SSSR, 1960.

Forestry Commission. <u>Conversion Tables for Research Workers in Forestry and Agriculture</u>. Booklet No. 5. London: Her Majesty's Stationery Office, 1965.

Fox, K. A. "A Spatial Equilibrium Model of the Livestock-Feed Economy in the United States." <u>Econometrica</u>, XXI (1953), 547-566.

Friedrich, C. J., ed. <u>Alfred Weber's Theory of the Location of Industries</u>. Chicago: University of Chicago Press, 1929.

Geller, M. S. <u>Programma Resheniya Na EBM "Minsk-2" zadachi Nakhozhdeniya Kratchayshikh Rasstoyaniy, Sebestoyimosti i Tarifov Na Transportnoy Seti</u>. Minsk, 1964.

Glotov, V. V. <u>Primeneniye Lineynogo Programmirovaniya v Lesnoy Promyshlennosti</u>. Moscow: Lesnaya Promyshlennost', 1965.

--------, <u>et al</u>. <u>Spravochnik po Ekonomike Lesnoy Promyshlennosti</u>. Moscow: Lesnaya Promyshlennost', 1967.

Goldman, T. A. "Efficient Transportation and Industrial Location." <u>Papers and Proceedings of the Regional Science Association</u>, IV (1958), 91-106.

Gorovoy, V. L. "The Timber Industry of Northern European Russia." <u>Soviet Geography</u> (April, 1961), 53-59.

--------. "Lesnye Resursy SSSR i ikh Ispol'zovaniye." <u>Geografiya SSSR</u>. Vypusk 1: <u>Zemel'nye Resursy i Lesnye Resursy SSSR</u>. Edited by I. I. Parkhomenko. Moscow: AN SSSR, 1965.

Gorovoy, V. L. and G. A. Privalovskaya. <u>Geografiya Lesnoy Promyshlennosti SSSR</u>. Moscow: Nauka, 1966.

Greenhut, M. L. <u>Plant Location in Theory and in Practise</u>. Chapel Hill: University of North Carolina Press, 1956.

Guchek, T. S., compiler. <u>Bibliografiya Po Voprosam Razmeshcheniya i Rayonirovaniya Promyshlennosti SSSR (1958-1964)</u>. Moscow: Nauka, 1966.

Guthrie, J. A. <u>The Economics of Pulp and Paper</u>. Pullman, Washington: State College of Washington Press, 1950.

Haden-Guest, S., <u>et al</u>. <u>A World Geography of Forest Resources</u>. Special Publication No. 33. New York: American Geographical Society, 1956.

Hardt, J. P., <u>et al</u>., eds. <u>Mathematics and Computers in Soviet Economic Planning</u>. New Haven and London: Yale University Press, 1967.

Hardwick, W. G. "Geography of the Forest Industry of Coastal B.C." <u>Occasional Papers in Geography</u>, Canadian Association of Geographers, B.C. Division, No. 5 (1963).

Henderson, J. M. <u>The Efficiency of the Coal Industry: An Application of Linear Programming</u>. Cambridge: Harvard University Press, 1958.

Hitchcock, F. L. "The Distribution of a Product from Several Sources to Numerous Localities." <u>Journal of Mathematics and Physics</u>, XX (1941), 224-230.

Holowacz, J. <u>Opportunities for Export of Paper Bags to the USSR</u>. Research Branch, Ontario Dept. of Lands and Forests. Ontario Government, February, 1964.

--------. "Organization, Production and Development of the Soviet Forest Industry."
Pulp and Paper Magazine of Canada, August, 1963, Feature Section.

Hooson, D. J. M. The Soviet Union. London: University of London Press Ltd., 1966.

Hoover, Edgar M. The Location of Economic Activity. New York: McGraw-Hill Inc., 1963.

Itogi Vsesoyuznoy Perepisi Naseleniya 1959, SSSR. Moscow: Gosstatizdat, 1961.

Itogi Vypolneniya Narodnokhozyaystvennogo Plana SSSR i Soyuznykh Respublik v 1964 godu.
Moscow: Statistika, 1965.

Katkoff, V. "Timber Industry of the USSR." Economic Geography, XVI (October, 1940),
390-406.

Katsenelenbaum, A. Z., chief ed. Spravochnik Ekonomista-Bumazhnika. Moscow: Lesnaya Promyshlennost', 1967.

Kitayev, I. V., et al. Produktsiya Khimicheskoy i Khimiko-Mekhanicheskoy Pererabotki
Drevesiny, Spravochnik. 2nd ed. Moscow: Lesnaya Promyshlennost', 1966.

Koch, A. R. and M. M. Snodgrass. "Linear Programming Applied to Location and Product Flow Determination in the Tomato Processing Industry." Papers and Proceedings
of the Regional Science Association, V (1959), 151-162.

Koopmans, T. C. "Optimum Utilization of the Transportation System." Cowles Commission Papers, New Series, No. 34 (1951), 136-146.

Korneyev, A. M., chief ed. Promyshlennost' v Khozyaystvennom Komplekse Ekonomich-
eskikh Rayonov SSSR. Moscow: Nauka, 1964.

Kovalin, D. T., ed. Spravochnik Lesnichego. 2nd ed. Moscow: Lesnaya Promyshlennost',
1965.

Kuchurin, S. F. Tarify Zheleznykh Dorog SSSR. Moscow: Transzheldorizdat, 1957.

Lavrishchev, A. N. Ekonomicheskaya Geografiya SSSR. Moscow: Ekonomika, 1965.

Lesnaya Promyshlennost' (newspaper). No. 148, 1963, p. 2; No. 94, 1964, p. 1; No. 131,
1964, p. 4.

Lösch, A. The Economics of Location. Translated by W. G. Woglom and W. F. Stolper.
New York: John Wiley & Sons, Inc., 1967.

Lydolph, P. E. Geography of the USSR. New York: J. Wiley & Sons, Inc., 1964.

Mellor, R. E. H. Geography of the USSR. London: Macmillan and Co. Ltd., 1964.

Mel'tser, E. M. and A. Ya. Eliashberg, compilers. Lesotekhnicheskiy Russko-Anglo-
Nemetsko-Frantsuzskiy Slovar' (Po Bumage i Lesu). Moscow: Lesnaya Promyshlennost', 1964.

Michalowicz, A. Z. "Interregional Comparison of the Transportation Costs of Newsprint." Unpublished M.Sc. Thesis, Forestry Faculty, University of Toronto, April,
1963.

Morrill, R. L. and W. L. Garrison. "Projections of Interregional Patterns of Trade in
Wheat and Flour." Economic Geography, XXXVI (April, 1960), 116-126.

132

Narodnoye Khozyaystvo Estonskoy SSR. Talin, 1957.

Narodnoye Khozyaystvo Latviyskoy SSR. Riga, 1957.

Narodnye Godpodarstvo Ukrainskoy RSR v 1960 rots¦. Kiev: 1965.

Narodnye Godpodarstvo Ukrainskoy RSR v 1964 rotsi. Kiev: 1965.

Narodnoye Khozyaystvo RSFSR v 1958 godu. Moscow: Gosstatizdat, 1959.

Narodnoye Khozyaystvo RSFSR v 1961 godu. Moscow: Gosstatizdat, 1962.

Narodnoye Khozyaystvo RSFSR v 1964 godu. Moscow: Statistika, 1965.

Narodnoye Khozyaystvo RSFSR v 1965 godu. Moscow: Statistika, 1966.

Narodnoye Khozyaystvo SSSR v 1958 godu. Moscow: Gosstatizdat, 1959.

Narodnoye Khozyaystvo SSSR v 1959 godu. Moscow: Gosstatizdat, 1960.

Narodnoye Khozyaystvo SSSR v 1961 godu. Moscow: Gosstatizdat, 1962.

Narodnoye Khozyaystvo SSSR v 1964 godu. Moscow: Statistika, 1965.

Nauchno-Issledovatel'skiy Institut Ekonomiki Stroitel'stva Gosstroya SSSR. Metodicheskiye Ukazaniya Po Opredeleniyu Optimal'nykh Skhem Perevozok, Snabzheniya i Razmeshcheniya Predpriyatiy s Pomoshch'yu Lineynogo Programirovaniya. Moscow: Ekonomika, 1964.

Nechuyatova, N. P. Geograficheskoye Razmeshcheniye Derevoobrabatyvayushchey Promyshlennosti SSSR. Moscow: G. L. B. I., 1963.

Nevzorov, N. V. Osnovy i Puti Razmeshcheniya Lesozagotovitel'noy Promyshlennosti v SSSR. Moscow: G. L. B. I., 1959.

Nikitin, N. P., ed. Ekonomicheskaya Geografiya SSSR. Moscow: Prosveshcheniye, 1966.

Nikolaev, S. "Principles of Construction for an Interzonal Model in a Soviet Setting." Papers, Regional Science Association, XX (1968), 135-139.

Oblomskiy, Ya. A. "Novoye Moshchnoye Orudiye Planirovaniya." Ekonomicheskaya Gazeta, No. 25 (1968), 11.

Panshin, A. J., et al. Forest Products, Their Sources, Production and Utilization. 2nd ed. New York: McGraw-Hill, 1962.

Pechat' SSSR v 1964 godu, Statisticheskiye Materialy. Moscow: Kniga, 1965.

Pechat' SSSR v 1965 godu, Statisticheskiye Materialy. Moscow: Kniga, 1966.

Perepechin, B. M. and N. P. Filinov. Lesopolzovaniye v SSSR 1946-1962. Moscow: Lesnaya Promyshlennost', 1962.

Ponomarev, A. D. "Lesnoy Fond SSSR." Lesnoye Khozyaystvo, XVI, No. 6 (1963), 48-55.

Power, G. C, "An Analysis of Geographical Factors Determining the Northern Limits of the Pulp and Paper Industry in Northern Ontario." Unpublished Masters thesis, McGill University, August, 1959.

Preyskurant No. 10-01, Tarifov na gruzovye zheleznodorozhnye perevozki. Moscow: Transzheldorizdat, 1960.

Prokhorchuk, I. S. Geograficheskoye Razmeshcheniye Bumazhnoy Promyshlennosti. Leningrad, 1939.

Promyshlennost' RSFSR. Moscow: Gosstatizdat, 1961.

Promyshlennost' SSSR. Moscow: Statistika, 1964.

"Put Out the Bonfire." Current Abstracts of the Soviet Press, I, No. 1 (1968), 7.

Referativny Zhurnal, No. 7 (1966).

Rodgers, Allan. "Changing Locational Patterns in the Soviet Pulp and Paper Industries." Annals, Association of American Geographers, XLV, No. 1 (1955), 85-104.

RSFSR v Tsifrakh v 1965 godu. Moscow: Statistika, 1966.

Shabad, Theodore. "Cost factor now dominant in Soviet resource development program." The Globe and Mail. October 31, 1967, p. 8. (Reprinted from The New York Times.)

Skhema Zheleznykh Dorog SSSR. Moscow: SSSR Ministerstvo Putey Soobshcheniya, 1963.

Smirnov, A. V. Perspektivy Razvitiya Fanernoy i Spichechnoy. Promyshlennosti v 1959-1965 gg. Moscow: G. L. B. I., 1960.

Smith, D. M. "A Theoretical Framework for Geographic Studies of Industrial Location." Economic Geography, XLII (April, 1966), 95-113.

Solecki, J. J. "Competition from Russia." Prepared for the seminar, "British Columbia's Future in Forest Products Trade in the Asia and Pacific Area." Vancouver, B.C., February 19, 1965.

--------. "Forest Resources and Their Exploitation in the USSR." Forestry Chronicle XXXIX (June, 1963), 212-222.

--------. "The Pulp and Paper Industry in the Soviet Union." Canadian Pulp and Paper Industry, XVIII, No. 8 (1965), 36-39, 54-55; ibid., No. 9 (1965), 35-39, 53.

Solecki, J. J. and J. A. Crosse. Soviet Forestry. Proceedings of Inter-Faculty Seminar on Forest Reserves in the USSR and their Utilization, November 1961-February 1962. Vancouver: Faculty of Forestry, University of British Columbia, 1963. (Mimeographed.)

Soviet Union Today. October, 1966.

Stepanov, P. N. Geografiya Promyshlennosti SSSR. Moscow: Uchpedgiz, 1955.

Suchil'nikov, N. G. Ekonomika Lesoobrabatyvayushchey Promyshlennosti. Moscow: G. L. B. I., 1961.

Titkov, P. E. and S. I. Kantor. "Transport i Spetsializatsiya Proizvodstva." Lesnaya Promyshlennost', XLII (November, 1962), 26-27.

Transport i Svyaz' SSSR. Statisticheskiy Sbornik. Moscow: Statistika, 1967.

Tseplyaev, V. P. Lesnoye Khozyaystvo SSSR. Moscow: Lesnaya Promyshlennost', 1965.

Uchastkina, Z. V. Ekonomika Tsellyulozno-Bumazhnoy Promyshlennosti. Moscow: G. L. B. I., 1963.

Uchastkina, Z. V. and G. B. Kasparov. Ekonomika, Organizatsiya i Planirovaniye Tsellyulozno-Bumazhnogo Proizvodstva. 2nd ed. Moscow: Lesnaya Promyshlennost', 1966.

U. S. Department of Commerce. Transportation Factors in the Marketing of Newsprint. Washington, D. C.: Government Printing Office, 1952.

Vasil'yev, P. V. Ekonomika Ispol'zovaniya i Vosproizvodstva Lesnykh Resursov. Moscow: AN SSSR, 1963.

--------. "Forestry in the USSR." Unasylva, XII, No. 2 (1958), 63-66.

--------. "Lesnye Resursy i Lesnoye Khozyaystvo." Prirodnoye Resursy Sovetskogo Soyuza. Moscow: AN SSSR, 1963.

--------. "Prospects for Industrial Consumption of Wood and for Development of the Forest Economy in the USSR under the Seven Year Plan (1959-1965)." Journal of Forestry, LVII (1959), 818-821.

--------. "USSR Forest Resources and Features of their Inventory." Unasylva, XV, No. 3 (1961), 119-124.

Vasil'yev, P. V. and A. G. Zheludkov. "Problemy Uluchsheniya Otraslevoy Struktury i Razmeshcheniya Lesnoy Promyshlennosti." Voprosy Razmeshcheniya Proizvodstva v SSSR. Edited by N. N. Nekrasov. Moscow: Nauka, 1965.

Vasil'yev, P. V., et al. Ekonomika Lesnogo Khozyaystva SSSR. 2nd ed. Moscow: Lesnaya Promyshlennost', 1965.

Vedushchev, A. I. Problemy Razmeshcheniya Proizvoditel'nykh Sil SSSR. Moscow: Ekonomicheskaya Literatura, 1963.

Verkhovskiy, B. S. and B. I. Shibalov. "Mnogoproduktovaya Model' s Ogranichivayushchim Resursom (Na Primere Bumazhnoy Promyshlennosti)." Matematicheskiye Metody i Problemy Razmeshcheniya Proizvodstva. Edited by I. Ya. Birman and L. E. Mints. Moscow: Ekonomicheskaya Literatura, 1963.

Vneshnaya Torgovlya SSSR za 1964 god. Moscow: Vneshtorgizdat, 1965.

Yarmola, I. S. Voprosy Lesosnabzheniya v SSSR. Moscow: Lesnaya Promyshlennost', 1966.

Zheleznye Dorogi SSSR, Napravleniya i Stantsii. 2nd ed. Moscow: Ministerstvo Geologii SSSR, 1966.

135

Soc
HD
9765
R9
1334

DATE